The Little Book of Stock Inve$ting

by
John Bajkowski
and
Maria Crawford Scott

041172\

Library of Congress number: 95-76306

ISBN: 0-943641-67-1

All Chapters were co-authored by John Bajkowski and Maria Crawford Scott and first appeared in the *AAII Journal*.

Table of Contents

4: A Basic Strategy: Dividend Yield Valuation 33

5: Growth Stock Investing 47

6: Investing in Utilities for Income and Growth 61

1

Fundamental Analysis Basics

One of the biggest difficulties for individuals interested in investing in stocks is getting started.

Entire books have been written about each and every aspect of fundamental stock analysis. These books walk investors through the fine details of corporate financial statements, comparative financial ratios, all kinds of stock screens, and every imaginable valuation model. The detail and complexity often leaves newcomers perplexed, wondering: Where do I begin, what is important, and how do I apply it to my situation?

In *The Little Book of Stock Inve$ting*, we will provide a general outline for analyzing stocks and walk through the process as it is practically applied to specific types of investment approaches. To achieve this without getting bogged down in details, we will use a somewhat simplistic approach. In the end you should have a general understanding of fundamental stock analysis and its practical application; from that base you can build up your knowledge of the details because in the real world marketplace you will be competing with those who know all of the details.

This chapter will describe, in very broad terms, the basic process followed in fundamental analysis.

Future chapters will go into more detail and show how the various steps can be adapted and practically applied to an individual's specific approach using commonly used published information sources.

The Basic Process

When buying a stock, an investor faces the same question that the purchaser of any good faces: Is this good worth the price being asked? Judging the worth or value of a stock is the basic aim of stock analysis. And to reach this aim using a fundamental approach, stock analysis follows this basic process:

- Since it isn't practical to judge the worth of every single stock in existence, you must start with a limited list of stocks that are promising investment candidates. How do you come up with this list? You might simply start with one or several stocks that someone has recommended, or that for one reason or other piqued your interest. A more methodical approach is to start with a list of stocks that have met certain criteria you set.
- Once you have a manageable-sized list to work with, you must gather information on and analyze the financial condition of the individual companies.
- The analysis of the firm's financial condition allows you to form expectations concerning its future; based on these expectations, you can put a

price on the stock—the amount you feel the stock is worth.

• Your final decision is based on how your estimated valuation compares with the current price of the stock. This may also be tempered by how confident you are with the information you have received, your analysis, and your expectations.

This short outline, described in lay terms, is reasonable, logical, and easier said than done.

Let's look at a more formal description of the outline, using investment terms for the steps of the process. Not only will this help you better understand the process, it may also help you identify areas you have read about or learned previously, but were unclear as to where they fit in the overall stock analysis process.

Initial Investment Criteria and Stock Screening

Aside from relying on recommendations, the primary method investors use to develop their initial manageable list of promising stocks is to concentrate on stocks with certain fundamental attributes.

Stock screens are simply criteria that are applied to a broad universe of stocks; the investor can then focus on the narrower list of stocks that pass the criteria. Screening involves scanning through a large universe of stocks, which is best done on a computer. Investors who don't use computers can use pre-screened lists that are available, or they can develop a set of criteria that stocks must meet before they are considered as candidates.

Obviously, the criteria by which stocks are initially selected are crucial. For the most part, these criteria will be based on your return objectives, tolerance for risk and investment philosophy.

Return objectives encompass not only the total return but how those returns are achieved—whether solely from price appreciation or a combination of price appreciation and dividend income.

Risk tolerance refers to how much volatility of return you can tolerate without panicking.

And *investment philosophy* encompasses the style used to select stocks; it is based in large part on your beliefs as to what drives stock prices. For instance, an investor with a tolerance for greater risk and few income needs may choose criteria that allow him to focus on growth-oriented companies, while an investor with a need for some income and less tolerance for risk may concentrate on stocks with higher dividends and lower price volatility, focusing, for example, on utilities with above-average dividend growth rates. This defines your overall investment approach.

Financial Statement and Ratio Analysis

Fundamental analysis is premised on the notion that the value or worth of a stock is based in large part on expectations concerning the future performance of the company. Since most investors lack a crystal ball, expectations are derived from a study of the past and current financial condition of the company and its ability to produce earnings.

Corporate financial statements are a key source for evaluating a company's financial condition. However, it's difficult to draw conclusions based solely on the raw numbers—for instance, learning that XYZ had net earnings of $19 million in 1992 doesn't add much to an understanding of the firm.

Ratio analysis is the method by which information from the various financial statement accounts can be assessed. Financial ratios are computed from selected information in the annual financial statements; examples that you may be familiar with already include the *current ratio* (current assets divided by current liabilities, a measure of the firm's ability to meet short-term obligations and operating expenses); *return on equity* (net profit after taxes divided by stockholders' equity, a measure of profitability), and *price-earnings ratio* (market price divided by earnings per share, a measure of how the market is currently pricing the stock).

A firm's financial ratios are compared to its historical ratios as well as industry ratios. Comparing financial ratios to historical ratios helps identify important trends, while comparing financial ratios to industry averages allows investors to see how the firm stacks up to competitors. This analysis allows investors to form judgments of the company upon which reasonable expectations can be built.

Stock Valuation

The goal of stock analysis is to determine a stock value that can be compared to the current market price. Stock valuation is aimed at formulating expectations about the company's future prospects and the potential risk and return behavior of the stock, and converting these expectations into a dollar value through the use of the proper valuation formula.

In practical terms, a stock's risk and return potential is based on expectations of earnings, dividends, cash flow, and asset values. While each of these is interrelated and interdependent, most valuation formulas usually concentrate on one variable. For the individual investor, valuation formulas based on assets or cash flows are difficult because it is difficult to obtain and analyze meaningful data. Information on earnings and dividends, however, is more readily available and presents the most practical base to build upon.

If all companies had similar financial conditions and operated in similar environments, an investor could use one valuation formula in every situation. However, companies differ in factors such as their stages of development, competitive nature, and industry. Certain valuation models are more appropriate for certain firms than they are for others. Stock valuation requires investor judgment at many levels, from determining which valuation models are appropriate for a particular firm, to determining the most reasonable assumptions to use in the formulas—for instance, should future growth expectations be based on a firm's expected dividend, sales or earnings growth?

The Actual Decision

Your final decision to invest in a stock will be based on a comparison of the stock's current market price to the value you have placed on the stock. And whether your decision was a good one is obviously dependent on all of the inputs—how promising your initial list was, how accurate the information you compiled on the firm was, how reasonable the assumptions and expectations you developed and used in your valuation formulas were, and whether or not you used appropriate assumptions and formulas in your analysis.

Applying the Basic Approach

How do you apply this process? As we have seen, determining the initial selection criteria depends heavily on an individual's investment philosophy, risk tolerance, and return needs—an individual's overall investment approach. But it's difficult to develop an approach without an understanding of what drives stock prices and valuations.

For that reason, Chapter 2 will take a look at a very basic financial statement, ratio analysis, and stock valuation form, to help give you a feel for the driving forces behind stock prices.

Chapter 3 will look at the various investment approaches, the types of investors who may be drawn to these approaches, and the risk, return, and other characteristics of stocks that are initially selected using these approaches.

Later chapters apply that basic form to various investment approaches, discussing which screens or criteria can be applied to draw up an initial list, which financial ratios should be emphasized, which valuation methods are most appropriate, sources of information, and special factors that should be taken into consideration.

The Little Book of Stock Inve$ting won't turn you into a financial analyst, but it should give you a foundation upon which to build a practical stock portfolio.

2

Getting Started

Stock selection requires you to gather and analyze data and information in a systematic way.

The task of selecting stocks is made easier by organizing the decision process to ensure that salient data and information is evaluated in some logical sequence that allows an investor to make a reasonable decision.

The ultimate goal is to determine, through a range of values, what you think the stock is really worth.

Let's run through a simplified version of the process.

The worksheet in Figure 2-1 provides an easy-to-follow systematic format that allows you to walk through the complete process without getting bogged down in complicated financial analysis. However, any final real-world decision would include the further evaluation of other fundamental aspects of the company.

At the bottom of the worksheet, two valuation models are presented, one based on a firm's earnings and the other on its dividends.

The two formulas look different, but they are actually quite similar except for the use of earnings in one and dividends in the other. They equate a

Figure 2-1: Valuation Worksheet

Company: _____   Current Price $ _____   Date (/ /)

Ticker _____ Exchange _____   Current P/E _____   Current Yield _____

Financial Statement & Ratio Analysis

Per Share Information	Company					Industry or Competitor		Market
	19___	19___	19___	19___	5-year avg	19___	5-year avg	19___
Price: High								
Price: Low								
Earnings per Share (EPS)					growth rate:			
Dividends per Share (DPS)					growth rate:			
Book Value per Share (BV)								
Financial Ratios								
Price-Earnings Ratio (P/E): Avg*								
High *(High Price ÷ EPS)*								
Low *(Low Price ÷ EPS)*								

Dividend Yield % (DY): Avg*							
Høgh *(DPS ÷ Low Price)*							
Low *(DPS ÷ High Price)*							
Payout Ratio % (DPS ÷ EPS)							
Return on Equity % (EPS ÷ BV)							
Financial Leverage %							

Avg = (High + Low) ÷ 2   *Shaded areas do no need to be filled in.*

Valuation Estimates

Model based on earnings:

Average high P/E × estimated 19___ EPS: _____ × _____ = _____ (high valuation estimate)

Average low P/E × estimated 19___ EPS: _____ × _____ = _____ (low valuation estimate)

Model based on dividends:

Estimated 19___ annual DPS ÷ average low DY**: _____ ÷ _____ = _____ (high valuation estimate)

Estimated 19___ annual DPS ÷ average high DY**: _____ ÷ _____ = _____ (low valuation estimate)

**Use decimal form for DY. For instance 5.4% would be 0.054.

stock's price to a stream of future earnings or dividends by asking the question: How much are investors paying for this expected stream?

Both models assume that the growth prospects of the firm have not changed fundamentally over time. The historical relationships between the stock's price and earnings or dividends per share can be used to estimate future value. Then, if current market prices differ significantly from the estimated values based on the historical relationships, it means the market, for whatever reason, is evaluating future income potential differently and may be mispricing the security.

Valuation Methods

The first approach—the price earnings ratio—is for stocks with low or non-existent dividends—the traditional growth stock. The price-earnings ratio—share price divided by earnings per share—indicates how much investors are willing to pay for each dollar of the firm's earnings. The higher the ratio, the more investors are paying for earnings, with the expectation that those earnings will increase, or the more confident they are of earnings predictions. Conversely, lower ratios indicate low earnings expectations, or a low confidence in earnings predictability.

For the earnings valuation, the average annual high and low price-earnings ratios are calculated for prior years. Multiplying these historical ranges by an estimate of next year's earnings per share provides an estimate of future value.

While it may seem difficult to make an earnings estimate, the recent earnings history that is part of the worksheet will give you some basis for forming those expectations. In addition, there are a number of sources where you can obtain analysts' estimates of future earnings, including Value Line and Standard & Poor's Corporation Records.(Appendix A in the back of the book provides an extensive listing of information sources.)

The second approach is primarily for mature, dividend-paying stocks, such as public utilities, which are generally low-growth stocks. It is a dividend yield approach. Dividend yield—dividends per share divided by share price—is the dividend as a percentage of the stock price. It relates share price to dividends; the *lower* the dividend yield, the greater the expectations are for dividend growth, or the more confident investors are in the predictability of dividends. The *higher* the dividend yield, the lower expectations are for dividend growth, or the lower the confidence in dividend predictability.

This approach requires an estimate of the next expected annual cash dividend. Again, the recent dividend history in the worksheet should provide you with a feel for changes over time, or you can use analysts' estimates.

Dividing the expected annual dividend by the average low dividend yield will give a high-price estimate; dividing the expected annual dividend by the average high dividend yield results in the low-price estimate.

Filling in the Numbers

To work through the equations at the bottom of the worksheet, you need to fill out the top section. This section—the Financial Statement and Ratio Analysis—collects the information needed in the valuation models, and also provides figures that will serve as a financial checklist. This financial checklist helps analyze the assumptions upon which the model is based, since if these assumptions are incorrect, your valuations are invalid.

The figures and ratios can be gathered using a company's financial statements, which means you will have to calculate many of the ratios yourself. A better bet, particularly for a beginner, is to use one of the various stock information sources that do much of the legwork for you.

The first section indicates per share information concerning the stock: the high and low share prices for the last five years, as well as earnings per share and dividends per share for each of the last five years. For the earnings per share and dividends per share figure, it is also useful to determine the five-year growth rate. In Chapter 3, we will discuss how this can be calculated. This growth rate can then be used to develop your own estimate of next year's earnings and dividends.

The next section lists financial ratios; here, the two primary ratios we are focusing on are the price-earnings ratio and dividend yield. For this model, these two figures should be calculated from the per share data: for price-earnings ratios, divide the high and low share price by the earnings per share; for dividend yield, divide the annual cash dividends by the high and low price. Averages are obtained by adding the yearly figures and dividing by the number of years with valid figures. Note that if earnings are negative or dividends nonexistent, you will be unable to calculate a figure for that year.

Also listed in this form is the payout ratio (dividends per share divided by earnings per share); return on equity (earnings per share divided by book value per share), and financial leverage (such as long-term debt to capitalization or long-term debt to equity), which are used as part of your financial checklist. Most of these ratios can be calculated from the per share financial data on the worksheet, or be taken from stock information sources. Financial leverage cannot be calculated by the per share data, and the various sources use different measures. For these reasons, it is important to stick to one information source when making comparisons.

Financial ratios for the industry in which the firm operates (or a close competitor) as well as for the market as a whole, are listed as well as part of the checklist.

The Financial Checklist

It's easy to compare the valuations you come up with to the current market price. But those valuations are only as good as the inputs and assumptions used in formulating the models.

For instance, the models assume that the firm's growth prospects have not fundamentally changed. But will growth continue at its current pace? The models also assume that historical relationships will continue. But were past relationships affected by a one-time occurrence that is unlikely to continue?

Will dividends continue to be paid at the same rate?

Examining the historical patterns of the per share figures and ratios, and comparing them to competitors and industry and market benchmarks, is particularly useful in evaluating your inputs and assumptions.

What do you look for and compare? In the worksheet, answering the following questions would be appropriate:

- Have earnings grown at a stable rate?
- Have the earnings per share been steady and positive each year, or have they been volatile, making predictions more difficult?
- For dividend-paying firms, has the payout ratio been steady? Increases in the payout ratio, and negative payout ratios, are an indication that future dividends may go down; high payout ratios mean

slower or no dividend growth, and perhaps even a decline.

- Is the current price-earnings ratio low relative to the market and industry or a competitor, and does this vary from previous years?
- Is the current dividend yield high relative to the market and industry or a competitor, and does this vary from previous years?
- Has the return on equity, a measure of financial return that provides an indication of how well the firm has used reinvested earnings to generate additional earnings, been high and stable?
- Is the use of financial leverage, a measure of financial risk that indicates how much of the assets of the firm have been financed by debt, low relative to industry norms?

Ameritech: An Example

Using Ameritech, with information reported by Value Line, helps illustrate the use of this simple worksheet. The per share information is presented in Table 2-1, along with some selected ratios. All figures have been adjusted, by Value Line, for a 2-for-1 stock split that occurred January 24, 1994.

If you work through these numbers, you will see that the price-earnings ratio model determined a high price of $49.83, a low price of $35.94 and an average price of $44.38, while the dividend model produced a high of $43.91, a low of $34.83 and an

Table 2-1: Ameritech: An Example

	1990	1991	1992	1993	1994
Price High: ($)	34.9	34.9	37.0	45.6	43.1
Price Low: ($)	26.3	27.9	28.1	35.1	36.3
EPS ($)	2.37	2.32	2.51	2.67	3.07
DPS ($)	1.61	1.72	1.78	1.86	1.94
BV ($)	14.63	15.18	12.94	14.35	10.98

Value Line estimated 1995 EPS: $3.30
Value Line estimated 1995 DPS: $2.00

Financial Ratios

	Ameritech		Industry	
	1994	5-yr. Avg.	1994	5-yr. Avg
Price-Earnings Ratio (X)	13.2	13.4*	13.9	14.8**
Dividend Yield (%)	4.8	5.2*	4.9	4.7**
Payout Ratio (%)	63	69	66	69
Return on Equity (%)	28	19.5	20.4	16.5
Long-Term Debt to Capitalization	42.3	38.7	44.7	44.2

*An average of the 5-year high and 5-year low. **An average of the last 4 years. Source: Value Line average price of $39.37. [You may end up with slightly different numbers due to rounding.] The current price (as of June 30, 1995) is around $44: It's trading within the predicted range of the price-earnings model, but just above the range for the yield-based model.

Are the assumptions and figures used in the model reasonable? A run through the checklist evaluates this:

• Yearly earnings per share appear to be increasing in a fairly stable pattern (except for 1991), and all of the figures were positive. Value Line's estimate for 1995, however, shows a smaller percentage increase than in the past. Further analysis—and understanding Value Line's reasons for this change—would be useful to determine whether or not you agree with Value Line's assessment.

• Ameritech's payout ratio has generally decreased over time and is now below that of the industry. This should enable Ameritech to support its dividend payment or even increase the payment if earnings continue to grow.

• Ameritech's price-earnings ratio is low compared to both its industry and the market (the S&P 500's price-earnings ratio currently is 15.4). Its dividend yield is roughly equal to the industry average. The price-earnings ratio points to a situation in which the market has not put as much faith in Ameritech's growth capability as it has in Ameritech's industry competitors. Who are those competitors? In the Value Line industry comparisons, many are high-flying cellular stocks, which tend to have higher growth and higher price-earnings ratios.

• Ameritech's return on equity has been stable and currently exceeds its industry norm. However, Ameritech's long-term debt ratio (Value Line's measure of financial leverage) has increased recently. Fortunately, it is slightly lower than the industry average. Companies can boost return on equity by taking on more debt, but they increase their risk to shareholders in the process.

The financial checklist indicates that some of the assumptions in the model are reasonable, but some—such as the Value Line assumptions concerning dividend and earnings growth—should be examined in more detail. A lower 1995 earnings per share estimate would, of course, produce lower valuation estimates.

Conclusion

For this particular company, your search may stop here. For stocks that appear more promising, however, you would need to look at other fundamental aspects before any investment decision is made.

For a simple beginning, the worksheet will provide you with an easy-to-follow systematic approach to determining value. The basic format is to:

• Determine which valuation model best suits your needs.

- Determine which information you need to gather for those valuations.
- Determine which information you need to evaluate the assumptions and other inputs used in the models.

Clearly, your information sources play a critical role in the analysis. In the next chapter, we will take a closer look at sources of information, and some of the problems and differences you may encounter when using them.

3

Sources of Information for the Simplified Approach to Valuation

In the last chapter, we presented a simplified version of the valuation process, along with a worksheet with two valuation models, one based on a firm's earnings and the other on its dividends.

The worksheet provides a systematic approach to gathering information needed for the valuations. Clearly, the information sources play a critical role in the analysis. In this chapter, we take a closer look at sources of information and some of the problems and differences you may encounter when using them.

Per Share Data

Most of the information on the worksheet in Chapter 2 can be derived from the per share financial information detailed at the top. This consists of, for each of the last five years: high and low share prices, earnings per share, dividends per share and book value per share.

The primary source for this information is the firm's annual financial reports. Corporate annual reports will include both summary and detailed financial statements, although even more detailed financial statements are available in a separate report, the 10K. Both of these reports can be requested from the company.

The detailed financial reports include the standard balance sheets for the last two years listing company assets, liabilities, and shareholder equity; income statements for the last three years listing items such as revenue, expenses, dividend payments, and earnings; statements of shareholders' equity for the last three years, which tracks the flow of funds into and out of shareholders' equity including retained equity and proceeds from new stock issues or stock option plans; and cash flow statements for the last three years, which examine increases or decreases in cash based on company operations, investing activities, and financial activities.

Also included in the detailed reports—and highly important—are the notes that accompany the statements. The notes address factors such as whether there were any changes in accounting policies that may impact the statements; a breakdown of inventory; depreciation schedules for property, plant, and equipment; terms of capital leases; detailed tax expense reports; litigations; material business changes such as acquisitions, investments, and major commitments with other companies; and even a detailed breakdown of long-term debt.

The annual report will also include a summary table that could prove useful in filling out the valuation worksheet. These tables often cover a 5- or 10-year span and may include basic data such as earnings per share, dividends per share, and book value per share. Some annual reports will also list historical high and low stock prices. However, there is no consistent format for these tables, and the amount of information provided varies from firm to firm.

Investors should always closely examine corporate financial reports. However, because of accounting differences and other consistency problems, it can be difficult to compare the data from one company's financial report to that of another.

A better bet for the beginner is to use one of the various information sources that do much of the legwork and adjustments for you. You can then refer to the corporate financial reports to double-check these sources and answer questions that might arise from the data they present.

The information sources presented in Table 3-1 provide extensive information on the companies covered; while there are other sources of piecemeal information, the ones listed should present you with enough basic information to complete the simplified valuation worksheet. (For a complete listing of sources, see Appendix A at the back of the book.)

Problems You May Encounter

While these sources are useful, it is important to understand how the information service you are using derives its figures, especially for comparative purposes.

Table 3-1: Corporate Financial Information Sources

Moody's Handbook of Common Stock—Analyzes over 1,600 common stocks; presents 10 years of data. Includes some industry information.

Standard & Poor's Stock Reports—Company reports are found in volumes according to the exchange on which they are traded; presents 10 years of data.

Value Line Investment Survey—Analyses over 1,600 common stocks in the Standard Edition plus an additional 1,800 stocks in the Expanded Edition; presents 15 years of data in the Standard Edition; 10 years of date in the Expanded Edition. Includes industry information.

This is particularly important in the calculation of earnings per share, which is subject to some financial accounting manipulation. For instance, companies can have conservative accounting policies in which they depreciate assets relatively quickly, or take large allowances for bad debt, either of which leads to greater initial expense and consequently lower earnings.

The way the information service handles accounting differences can make a big difference. As an example, Value Line does not include non-recurring gains or losses in its calculations but instead chooses to footnote those amounts. Standard & Poor's, on the other hand, chooses to include extraordinary items in its reports, which makes it possible for the two services to come up with different historical growth rates for the same company.

Dividends are subject to less accounting differences than earnings, but the information services may handle extraordinary dividends differently.

In comparing companies, the date of the fiscal year-end can also have an impact. Most services report company annual data based upon the company fiscal year, which varies from company to company. The effect of fiscal year-end differences is sometimes magnified in times of economic turnaround or industry upheaval. Differences of only six months can have a major impact on the calculation of historical growth rates and ratios. The key is to know that such differences may exist, and to keep these in mind when comparing companies.

Because of these differences, it is probably best for beginners to stick to one information source when comparing companies.

Growth Rates and Estimates

The simplified valuation approach presented in Chapter 2 requires estimates of next year's earnings and dividends per share. You can either come up with your own estimates, based on an examination of past growth and a forecast of future company and industry prospects, or use outside information sources for estimates.

If you wish to use the historical growth rate as a guide to future earnings and dividends, you need to determine the historical growth rate over the past five years, using the historical per share data from the worksheet. The formula is presented in the equation in Figure 3-1.

Next year's earnings and dividends per share can then be estimated by multiplying the current year's earnings and dividends per share by 1.00 plus the growth rate in decimal form. (This formula is also presented in the equation in Figure 3-1).

Estimates of next year's earnings and earnings growth can also be obtained from outside sources such as Value Line, which derives its own estimates (and which also estimates dividends for the next year), or from consensus reports. In consensus reports, a large number of analysts are periodically polled and asked for their estimates of earnings per share for the next few years, along with estimates of long-term growth rates. Table 3-2 presents sources for these estimates.

Industry Information

Industry information for comparison purposes is available from a wide variety of sources, many of which are listed in Table 3-3. Some of these sources are expensive, so you may want to check with your local library.

Information on the overall "market" is available in many newspapers, but the most standard definition of the market is the Standard & Poor's 500 index. A few sources of information on the S&P 500 index are the **Standard & Poor's Outlook** and, for a longer-term view of the S&P Index, the **Standard & Poor's Security Price Index Record.**

Figure 3-1: Equation to Determine Growth Rate of Earnings Per Share (EPS) & Dividends Per Share (DPS)

$$(EV/BV)^{1/n} - 1.00 = g$$

Where:

	EV	= Ending value (latest EPS or DPS)
	BV	= Beginning value (earliest EPS or DPS)
	n	= Number of yearly periods
	g	= Growth rate in decimal form

Note that if you have five years of data, you will have only four yearly compounding periods. For instance, EPS and DPS figures for 1989, 1990, 1991, 1992 and 1993 represent four yearly periods: 1989-90, 1990-91, 1991-92 and 1992-93.

Equations to Estimate Next Year's EPS or DPS

$$EPS_{CY} \times (1.00 + g) = EPS_{est}$$

or

$$DPS_{CY} \times (1.00 + g) = DPS_{est}$$

Where:

	EPS_{CY} & DPS_{CY}	= Current year EPS & DPS
	EPS_{est} & DPS_{est}	= Next year's estimated EPS & DPS
	g	= Growth rate in decimal form

Table 3-2: Sources of Earnings Estimates

Independent Investors Research Inc.

Analyst Watch

Institutional Broker's Estimate System (I/B/E/S)

Nelson's Earnings Outlook

Standard & Poor's Earnings Guide

Standard & Poor's Stock Reports

Value Line Investment Survey

See Appendix A for addresses and phone numbers.

Table 3-3: Sources for Industry Statistics

Almanac of Business and Industrial Financial Ratios—Provides financial ratios and operating factors for 181 industries classified in 16 categories. Published annually.

Barron's—A listing of the Dow Jones Industry Groups is given in the Market Statistics Section.

Dun & Bradstreet Industry Norms and Key Business Ratios—Calculates industry norms of financial statement items along with 14 key business ratios on 800 types of business, grouped in 4,000 asset and geographic industry segments.

Industriscope—Information on over 6,500 companies classified into 175 industry groups.

Investor's Business Daily—Investor's Business Daily Prices is presented every Tuesday and includes price changes in 197 industry indexes.

RMA Annual Statement Studies—Composite financial data for the most recent fiscal year is provided on approximately 350 industries.

Standard & Poor's Industry Surveys—Quarterly data is provided on 34 industries.

Standard & Poor's Analyst's Handbook—Reports the performance of over 70 industries as defined by the S&P subindexes.

Standard & Poor's Industry Reports—A monthly review of 80 industries.

Value Line Investment Survey—The Ratings and Reports volume (Part Three of the survey) presents composite statistics on each industry individually in various issues.

The Wall Street Journal—The Dow Jones Industry Groups is presented daily.

4

A Basic Strategy:
Dividend-Yield Valuation

In the first chapters we laid out the basic framework for building a stock portfolio.

We also examined a simplified approach for financial statement and ratio analysis and for stock valuation including a basic worksheet used to value prospective stocks based on two simple valuation models (one earnings-based and one dividend-based).

In the following chapters, we will show how to apply this simplified approach to various investment strategies using the basic sources of information identified in the last chapter.

In this chapter, the dividend yield valuation process will be discussed.

Developing the Initial Lists

A dividend-yield strategy can help find potentially undervalued stocks with low downside risk, provided the dividend is secure and expected to grow, and the firm is financially sound. This strategy will also tend to produce more income in the form of dividends, and less in the form of capital gains, than other strategies.

In the last chapter, we presented sources of information for financial statement and ratio analysis. These sources provide thorough, consistent and easy-to-compare information. But it would be difficult for an investor to go through each company page-by-page and compare dividend yields for thousands of companies.

For the beginning investor, there are other more useful sources from which you can draw your initial list of prospective candidates; a suggested list is presented in Table 4-1.

Most of the sources in Table 4-1 are inexpensive; they may also be available in your local library. Many of these sources do not present information that is sufficient or consistent (for instance, on a calendar-year basis) for the financial statement and ratio analysis that must be done later. In addition, several are published annually, so the information in them may become dated. However, they do provide a good starting point to narrow your search.

Be careful that you do not concentrate on a specific industry; you must be particularly careful using this strategy, since utilities and, to a lesser extent, financial companies will tend to dominate many of the lists. Since the approach works best with companies paying meaningful dividends, look for dividend yields of at least 2% or more. In addition, you should decide if you want to concentrate on absolute yield (is the dividend yield high compared to all other companies?), relative yield (is it high relative to its industry or to its historical average?), or perhaps both. This will help narrow the selection. Other conditions can help narrow the selection further—for instance, a low risk ranking or rating by one of the information sources.

Once a list of candidates is established the next step is to perform an in-depth evaluation of the selected stocks to determine the fair market value.

The following example is based on published information that was available in April of 1994, when the approach was applied.

Bristol-Myers Squibb: An Example

Bristol-Myers Squibb offers a good example of the dividend-yield approach: In mid-April of 1994, the firm was listed in S&P's table indicating it has paid higher cash dividends in each of the past 10 calendar years, and it was listed in Value Line's table of high-yielding non-utility stocks. Its dividend yield was 5.7% as of the end of March 1994.

In mid-April of 1994, Bristol-Myers Squibb, represented a fallen angel, a former growth company that had moved into a more mature, slower growth stage. It had popped up on the lists of high-yielding stocks because of concerns over both the industry and company. At that time, in comparison to the overall stock market, drug stocks had been weak performers since the beginning of 1992. Uncertainty surrounding changes to the nation's healthcare and its impact on the traditional drug manufacturers lead to devaluation of drug stocks

Table 4-1: Dividend-Yield Information Sources

Business Week—In late March or early April, *America's 1,000 Most Valuable Companies* is published, which presents the one-line statistical information and ratios—including dividend yield—on each firm. The magazine also includes summary statistics so individual firms can be compared against the average.

Moody's Handbook of Dividend Achievers—Includes information on 362 companies that have increased their dividends consistently over the past 10 years. The listings include a company's dividend achiever rank, as well as the company's dividend growth rate for the latest 10-year period.

Standard & Poor's 500 Guide, annual edition
Standard & Poor's MidCap 400 Guide, annual edition
Standard & Poor's SmallCap 600 Guide, annual edition—These guides include two useful lists: *Fast-Rising Dividends:* Firms whose dividend yields may not be at an absolute high, but show promise; *Higher Dividends for 10 Years:* Firms that have paid higher cash dividends in each of the past 10 years and whose dividend yield is currently at least 2%.

Standard & Poor's Earnings Guide—Includes one-line information and focuses on earnings, but the front includes one useful list: *Dividend Increases With Strong Coverage:* These are firms that have passed a fairly rigorous screen including increasing dividends, a payout ratio that has been between 10% and 90% for each of the last five fiscal years, and an average dividend coverage for five years that has been at least 1.7.

Continued

Table 4-1: Dividend-Yield
Information Sources, *Cont'd*

Standard & Poor's Industry Reports—Monthly review of 80 industries and some 900 stocks includes dividend yield percentages for each industry. In the back of these reports, there are one-line listings for selected companies within the industry. Listings include dividend yields.

Value Line Investment Survey—The front page lists median estimated yields of all stocks. The tables in the back include two useful lists: *High-Yielding Stocks:* This consists almost entirely of utilities. For this reason, you would not want to concentrate solely on this list; *High-Yielding Non-Utility Stocks:* Financial companies tend to dominate the list, but it is still useful. The listing also notes if dividend cuts are possible.

Also of Note:

Investment Quality Trends—Published twice monthly, each newsletter looks at the dividend yield of some 350 blue-chip stocks with high ratings and strong dividend-paying histories.

even though the short-term profit picture had not changed. In the long term, Value Line noted at the time that the industry, long regarded as a growth vehicle, could in a "worst-case scenario" go the way of regulated utilities.

Individual company concerns for Bristol-Myers Squibb included costs associated with settling cases dealing with silicone breast implants, fewer tax credits for manufacturing operations in Puerto Rico, as well as the normal drug firm concerns involving the loss of patent protection for drug products.

Figure 4-1 shows the completed valuation worksheet presented in Chapter 2. Value Line was used as the source of both company and industry information.

Entering the per share data from a source such as Value Line or S&P is a fairly straightforward process. The difficulty lies in determining the type of adjustments the data services made to provide the information. Value Line does not include nonrecurring items in its data. For 1993, Bristol-Myers had a $0.60 per share special charge for potential liabilities in connection with discontinued silicone implant operation, but this is only footnoted in the $4.40 earnings per share figure Value Line reports for 1993. Using the reduced $3.80 figure in the valuation worksheet would change the high and low price-earnings ratios for the year, the average price-earnings ratios, the earnings per share growth rate, payout ratio, return on equity and, ultimately, the valuation. Once you select a source for company information it is important to stick with it for all of the data elements, unless you know how to adjust the figures to make everything comparable.

Many analysts like to use dividends to value a company because of the purity of the dividend. The reported dividend paid is exactly what was paid, while management has some latitude in reported earnings figures. They may use liberal accounting principles to report higher earnings or decide to defer or take special charges to earnings until it works to their advantage.

A Tour of the Worksheet: Per Share Information

The first item that should strike you as you look at the price information is the change in trend that occurred between 1992 and 1993. Bristol-Myers' price peaked at just over $90 in early 1992, compared to a March 31, 1994 price of $51.50. This change coincided with weakness in the drug industry.

Next, it is important to examine the year-by-year dividend and earnings per share figures. Even though we are focusing on dividends, it is the profitability and cash generation of the firm that supports the dividend. First, examine the year-by-year figures—are they increasing, decreasing, or holding steady? Has there been a change in trend? Steady, increasing figures are best. Using the Value Line data, we see that earnings, dividends and book value have increased every year. The five-year average growth rates for earnings and dividends have been 12.5% and 9.5%, respectively. These are strong growth rates, but both earnings and dividends show some slowdown in their growth rates in the later years. Calculating the year-by-year percentage change for earnings and dividends is an effective tool for identifying changes in trends and growth rates.

Figure 4-1: Valuation Worksheet

Company: Bristol-Myers Squibb   **Current Price $** 51.50   **Date** (3 / 3 1/ 94)

Ticker BMY   **Exchange** NYSE   **Current P/E** 13.6   **Current Yield** 5.7%

Financial Statement & Ratio Analysis

	19_89	19_90	19_91	19_92	19_93	5-year avg	Industry or Competitor 19_93	Industry or Competitor 5-year avg	Market 19_93
Per Share Information									
Price: High	58.0	68.0	89.4	90.1	67.3				
Price: Low	44.0	50.5	61.1	60.1	50.9				
Earnings per Share (EPS)	2.75	3.33	3.95	4.07	4.40	*growth rate: 12.5%*			
Dividends per Share (DPS)	2.00	2.12	2.40	2.76	2.88	*growth rate: 9.5%*			
Book Value per Share (BV)	9.67	10.34	11.15	11.62	12.10				
Financial Ratios									
Price-Earnings Ratio (P/E): Avg	18.5	17.8	19.1	18.5	13.5	17.5	NA	18.3*	21.3
High (High Price ÷ EPS)	21.1	20.4	22.6	22.1	15.3	20.3			
Low (Low Price ÷ EPS)	16.0	15.2	15.5	14.8	11.6	14.6			

Dividend Yield % (DY); Avg	4.0	3.7	3.3	3.9	5.0	4.0	NA	2.5*	2.7
High (DPS ÷ Low Price)	4.5	4.2	3.9	4.6	5.7	4.6			
Low (DPS ÷ High Price)	3.4	3.1	2.7	3.1	4.3	3.3			
Payout Ratio % (DPS ÷ EPS)	72.7	63.3	60.7	67.8	65.4	66.0	44.0	45.6	
Return on Equity % (EPS ÷ BV)	28	32	35	35	36	33	30	29	
Financial Leverage** %	5	4	2	3	6	4	12	15	

*four-year averages. Value Line did not have 1993 industry figures for these items.   Grayed items were not needed for this valuation.
**long-term debt divided by equity.

Valuation Estimates

Model based on earnings:

Average high P/E × estimated 19 94 EPS: $\underline{20.3} \times \underline{4.70} = \underline{\$95.41}$ (high valuation estimate)
Average low P/E × estimated 19 94 EPS: $\underline{14.6} \times \underline{4.70} = \underline{\$68.62}$ (low valuation estimate)

Model based on dividends:

Estimated 19 94 annual DPS ÷ average low DY: $\underline{2.92} \div \underline{0.033} = \underline{\$88.48}$ (high valuation estimate)
Estimated 19 94 annual DPS ÷ average high DY: $\underline{2.92} \div \underline{0.046} = \underline{\$63.48}$ (low valuation estimate)

Use decimal form for DY. For instance 5.4% would be 0.054.

Looking at the Financial Ratios

Since our valuation of Bristol-Myers focuses on dividend yield, the portions of the worksheet pertaining to the price-earnings ratio and earnings valuation have been grayed out.

In the dividend analysis of a firm, the consideration of the safety of the dividend is of great concern. A high current yield itself does not mean that a stock is undervalued. It may indicate that the market feels that the dividend is in jeopardy. For a high relative current dividend yield to be considered a sign of an undervalued stock, the company must be expected to continue to pay and expand the dividend both this year and for years to come.

The payout ratio (dividends per share divided by earnings per share) is particularly useful in gauging the strength of the dividend. Generally, the lower the payout ratio, the more secure the dividend. Any ratio above 50% is considered a warning sign. However, like all ratios the payout ratio is industry-specific. Very stable industries, such as utilities, have high payout ratios, which is considered normal. A 100% payout ratio shows that a firm is paying out all of its earnings to its shareholders. Figures above 100% indicate that the payout is greater than earnings, a situation that cannot continue forever; while negative ratios show that a company is paying out a dividend while losing money.

Bristol-Myers Squibb has averaged a 66% payout ratio over the last five years, a figure higher than one would generally like to see. Beyond not having enough cash to cover the dividend payment, a policy of high dividend payout may limit future growth if capital expenditures and research and development are reduced to maintain the dividend. Drug firms are not capital-intensive, but they are research-intensive. Investment in research takes many years, if ever, to pay off.

Financial leverage is another indicator of dividend safety. Heavier debt loads saddle a company with required cash outflows to bondholders, who must be paid before dividends can be paid to shareholders. A company with little debt that runs into earnings problems has the ability to borrow. For Bristol-Myers, we used the ratio of long-term debt to equity as a measure of financial leverage. This figure was selected because comparable industry data was also available for this ratio. Bristol-Myers' ratio of 6% with a 4% five-year average is very low. This also compares favorably with the industry figures of 12% for 1993 and the industry's 15% five-year average. While the ratio of long-term debt to equity is a common ratio, it does possess some inherit weaknesses. The ratio does not consider short-term liabilities or other liabilities that are significant for Bristol-Myers. The ratio of total debt to total assets shows that liabilities are equal to about half of total assets, higher than the 34% figure for the drug industry.

It is the dividend yield portion of the financial ratio section that is of primary importance in the dividend valuation process. Looking at year-by-year figures shows an interesting change in trend. From

1989 to 1991, Bristol-Myer's dividend yield was trending down. This was a period of tremendous performance for the drug stocks. Since then the yield has risen steadily due to a dividend payout increase coupled with a stock price decline. The five-year average high and low yields are 4.6% and 3.3%, respectively, levels significantly below the current yield of 5.7%.

Valuing the Company

The bottom of the Valuation Worksheet provides valuations using the dividend-based model. Applying the model to Bristol-Myers paints an interesting picture. The first item that needs to be determined is the appropriate per share dividend for 1994. The worksheet uses Value Line's 1994 dividend estimate of $2.92, leading to a high valuation of $88.48 and low valuation of $63.48. This compares to a mid-April 1994 price of $51.50. But before you reach for the phone to call your broker, let's look at some of the assumptions behind the numbers.

The first area to consider is the dividend itself. The estimated 1994 figure of $2.92 represents an increase, although small, over the $2.88 dividend for 1993. If you were to expand last year's dividend by the historical growth of 9.5% you would get $3.15 [$2.88 x (1 + 0.095)], showing that $2.92 falls significantly short of the past trend. This figure even falls below Value Line's 8.5% estimate of dividend growth, and is the first signal of a change in trend. It is a good exercise to try different dividend estimates and see the impact on the valuation. If you think that a dividend cut is possible, try the valuation with the new dividend. A halving of the $2.88 dividend to $1.44 leads to a valuation range of $31.30 to $43.64, all else being equal.

The next area to look at is the average high and low dividend yields. In considering whether the five-year averages of 3.3% and 4.6% are appropriate numbers, you need to ask whether the fundamental characteristics of the company have changed and higher levels are appropriate. If you assume the government will start to further regulate the industry and set prices, then these drug firms may become more like utilities and trade with higher expected yields, coupled with lower growth rates and lower profit margins. Under this scenario the current price seems fair. Changing the required dividend yield to 6% leads to a valuation of $48.67 using the $2.92 dividend estimate.

By changing the required dividend yield determining the effect on valuation, you can quickly see that the stock price is even more sensitive to slight changes in yield than to changes in dividend.

Conclusion

Performing sensitivity analysis of this nature is a critical part of the valuation. It helps to provide you with a sense of the factors that drive a stock price and informs you of the factors to focus on when performing the valuation.

The worksheet focuses on the quantitative factors of valuation. Any final decision should also be based on a better understanding of the company, its management, and its competitive environment. This can only be accomplished by a thorough reading of the firm's financial reports, as well as the reports and summaries on the firm and its industry.

5

Growth Stock Investing

A growth approach to investing can help you find stocks with the potential for significant price appreciation, provided the firm is able to meet and exceed its growth expectations and you don't overpay for growth. This strategy produces very little return in the form of dividends and can be volatile because of the large role that expectations play in the pricing of these stocks.

Company Characteristics

Growth companies expand at a rate above that of the overall economy. Practically speaking, however, the minimum benchmark for being classified as a growth stock is at least a 10% annual growth rate in earnings per share, with many investors requiring a 20% annual growth rate. To maintain growth rates this high over any extended period, capital spending is required, and for this reason growth stocks tend to retain most of their earnings, paying little or no cash dividends.

Promising growth stocks attract a great deal of attention, and therefore prices tend to be bid up with high anticipation. High expectations relative to current levels of earnings lead to high price-earnings ratios, and it is not uncommon to see highly touted growth stocks with price-earnings ratios two to four times that of the market.

As long as the firm maintains its earnings per share momentum and exceeds the growth expectations of the market, its stock price can be expected to increase by quite a bit. However, a small deviation from market expectations during a quarterly earnings announcement can send the price flying in either direction. Thus, while growth stocks have the potential for high returns, they are also high risk.

The Initial List

The first step in the basic framework, of course, is drawing up an initial list of promising candidates for further analysis. A growth approach focuses initially on companies that consistently have had above-average earnings growth over the past few years.

For the beginning investor, there are several sources from which you can draw your initial list; some suggestions are presented in Table 5-1. Most of these sources are inexpensive and may also be available in your local library. These sources are useful primarily for the initial list—many of them do not present information that is sufficient or consistent for the financial statement and ratio analysis. In addition, several are published annually, so may become dated—a particular concern for growth investors, since quarterly earnings reports can produce unexpected surprises.

Again, do not concentrate on a specific industry. In addition, cyclical companies may turn up on growth lists at certain times if they are in an up-swing in their cycle. For this reason, make sure you examine earnings growth over longer time periods covering at least one economic cycle. Requiring consistently rising earnings each year can also help identify more stable growth companies. Other conditions can help narrow the selection fur-ther—for instance, eliminating companies with outrageous price-earnings ratios.

Once a list of candidates is established, the next step is to perform an in-depth evaluation of the stocks to determine the fair market value.

The following example is based on published information that was available in May of 1994, when the approach was applied.

Toys "R" Us: An Example

Toys "R" Us offers a good example of the growth approach: In mid-May of 1994, the firm was listed in the S&P Earnings Guide's list of rapid growth stocks, indicating it has actual and estimated five-year annual earnings growth rates of at least 10%. It also made Value Line's high growth stock list, indicating an average growth rate of 13% or more over the last 10 years and an estimated 13% or more growth rate in the next five years.

In mid-May of 1994, Toys "R" Us represented a growth company that continued its expansion

Table 5-1: Growth Approach Information Sources

BusinessWeek—In late May the magazine comes out with an issue that includes The Best Small Companies, a ranking of small firms (annual sales between $10 million and $150 million) based on three-year results in sales growth, earnings growth and return on invested capital. Includes a short description of each firm.

Standard & Poor's 500 Guide, annual edition
Standard & Poor's MidCap 400 Guide, annual edition
Standard & Poor's SmallCap 600 Guide, annual edition—These include two useful lists: *Companies With Five Consecutive Years of Earnings Increase:* Firms that have recorded rising earnings per share for five consecutive years, have a minimum 10% earnings per share growth rate based on trailing 12-month earnings, have estimated next year earnings per share at least 10% above those reported for the current year, pay dividends, and have S&P earnings and dividend rankings of A- or better; *Rapid Growth Stocks:* Firms that have shown strong and consistent earnings growth. These annual guides include the full-page data pages found in the S&P Stock Reports; since they are published annually, the data can be dated.

Continued

Table 5-1: Growth Approach Information Sources, *Cont'd*

Standard & Poor's Earnings Guide—Includes (one-line) information and focuses on earnings and earnings growth estimates. The front includes two short useful lists: *Rapid Growth Stocks:* These are firms that have been selected by S&P for superior earnings growth, with actual and estimated five-year annual earnings growth rates at least 10%; *High Rank, High Projected Growth Rate:* These firms carry high S&P rankings, have projected five-year earnings growth rates of at least 12%, are estimated to show earnings gains of at least 12% for each of the next two years, and have price-earnings ratios on estimated 1995 earnings of under 20.

Value Line Investment Survey—Part I Summary & Index: The tables in the back include this useful list: *High Growth Stocks:* This consists of firms with average growth rates of 13% or more over the last 10 years and estimated 13% or more growth in the next five years.

despite its large market capitalization. It had done so first by outmatching its competition, and then by expanding its markets. The toy retailer had more recently ventured into children's clothing (through its Kids "R" Us stores), mail catalog sales, action figure and video software products, and foreign operations.

The foreign markets area at that time was coming under increasing scrutiny in analysts' projections. In any growth company, a major concern is how the company can continue to expand. Toys "R" Us at that time dominated the retail U.S. toy market, with subsequently less room to expand, and the retail market itself is not a growth industry; the focus, therefore, was into expanding product lines such as children's clothing and books or by opening more stores overseas.

Figure 5-1 shows the completed valuation worksheet presented in Chapter 2. Value Line was used as the source of both company and industry information.

Entering the per share data from an information source is relatively straightforward. However, one potential source of confusion may come when trying to determine the actual years covered by the data reporting source. For example, Toys "R" Us has a fiscal year-end of January 31, which means that most of the activity for the firm will have taken place in the previous year. Value Line reports data for 1993 based on the January 31, 1994, fiscal year-end report. Standard & Poor's, on the other hand, reports 1993 data based on the January 31, 1993, fiscal year-end—which is 1992 data in Value Line's report.

A Tour of the Worksheet:
Per Share Information

The first item that may strike you is that the stock price that is "current" on the worksheet is nearly 20% below its all-time highs in 1993—double the market's decline from its high over the same time.

Toys "R" Us reacted in classical growth stock fashion: Its price took a fall after the first of the year because it only met—and failed to exceed—expected predictions for a strong Christmas season. Underlying the strong but expected domestic performance was lower than expected foreign sales.

Next, examine the year-by-year earnings per share figures. Are they steadily increasing, or has there been a change in trend? Earnings are clearly increasing, but the biggest increase occurred in 1992 when earnings shot up 27.8%. Calculating the year-by-year percentage change for earnings is an effective tool for identifying changes in trends and growth rates.

The Value Line data also shows an increase in book value every year.

Looking at the Financial Ratios

Toys "R" Us pays no dividend, and so the portions of the worksheet pertaining to dividend yield and dividend valuation are shaded. However, that doesn't mean that the company's dividend policy can't generate some useful insight.

Figure 5-1: Valuation Worksheet

Company: Toys "R" Us   **Current Price $** 34.62   **Date** (4 /29 / 94)

Ticker TOY   **Exchange** NYSE   **Current P/E** 21.2   **Current Yield** 0%

| | Financial Statement & Ratio Analysis | | | | | | Industry or Competitor | | Market |
| | Company | | | | | | | | |
Per Share Information	19.82	19.90	19.91	19.92	19.93	5-year avg	19.93	5-year avg	19.93
Price: High	26.80	35.00	36.00	41.00	42.90				
Price: Low	16.00	19.90	22.00	30.40	32.40				
Earnings per Share (EPS)	1.09	1.11	1.15	1.47	1.65	*growth rate:* 10.9%			
Dividends per Share (DPS)	0.00	0.00	0.00	0.00	0.00	*growth rate:* na			
Book Value per Share (BV)	5.95	7.11	8.39	9.85	11.6				
Financial Ratios									
Price-Earnings Ratio (P/E): Avg	19.6	24.7	25.2	24.3	22.8	23.3	19.0	17.9	21.3
High *(High Price ÷ EPS)*	24.6	31.5	31.3	27.9	26.0	28.3			
Low *(Low Price ÷ EPS)*	14.7	17.9	19.1	20.7	19.6	18.4			

Dividend Yield % (DY): Avg	0.0	0.0	0.0	0.0	0.0	0.0	1.0	1.1	2.7
High *(DPS ÷ Low Price)*	0.0	0.0	0.0	0.0	0.0	0.0			
Low *(DPS ÷ High Price)*	0.0	0.0	0.0	0.0	0.0	0.0			
Payout Ratio % (DPS ÷ EPS)	0.0	0.0	0.0	0.0	0.0	0.0	22.0	21.0	
Return on Equity % (EPS ÷ BV)	18.3	15.6	13.7	14.9	14.2	15.4	15.0	15.7	
Financial Leverage* %	10.1	9.5	16.1	23.2	19.5	15.6	30.4	34.1	

*long-term debt divided by equity.

Figures in gray were not needed for this valuation.

Valuation Estimates

Model based on earnings:

Average high P/E × estimated 19 94 EPS: $\underline{28.3}$ × $\underline{\$1.83}$ = $\underline{\$51.79}$ (high valuation estimate)

Average low P/E × estimated 19 94 EPS: $\underline{18.4}$ × $\underline{\$1.83}$ = $\underline{\$33.67}$ (low valuation estimate)

Model based on dividends:

Estimated 19 94 annual DPS ÷ average low DY: _____ ÷ _____ = _____ (high valuation estimate)

Estimated 19 94 annual DPS ÷ average high DY: _____ ÷ _____ = _____ (low valuation estimate)

Use decimal form for DY. For instance 5.4% would be 0.054.

Growth firms generally pay no dividends because they want to use capital for expansion. Toys "R" Us in spring of 1994, paid no dividends, but it had recently announced a buy-back of $1 billion worth of shares over the next few years. At a minimum this is a sign that the company is generating more cash than it feels it needs for future expansion. As companies first move to buy back shares and then pay cash dividends, they are indicating that new projects are not offering the same return potential to the company as once was the case. The move could be one sign that Toys "R" Us may be reaching a more mature stage—in other words, it may be turning into more of a mature company rather than a growth firm.

In a growth approach, the historical earnings growth rate provides one guide to future growth. But equally important are market expectations concerning future growth rates. Examining the price-earnings ratios are useful to judge market expectations concerning the future growth of the firm.

At 21.2, the current (mid-May 1994) price-earnings ratio of Toys "R" Us is edging toward the lower end of its historical range. It is still above the industry average, and close to the market's 1993 ratio—which is low for a growth stock. Traditionally the price-earnings ratio of a growth stock trades above that of the market and the Toys "R" Us ratio has traditionally been about 20% above the market's. While a low price-earnings ratio can be a sign of an undervalued stock, it can also be a sign that the market has lowered its expectations for the firm—it may no longer view the company as a true growth stock. It is worthwhile to consider whether the market may be correct in its assessment.

The 1993 return on equity for Toys "R" Us was below both the long-term average and the industry average. The return on equity measures how well the firm is being run on both an operational and financial basis. To boost return on equity a company must increase the profit margin on goods being sold, make better use of its assets, or increase the level of financial leverage. While the ratio is close to industry norms, the slide in return on equity for Toys "R" Us is surprising in light of the increase in financial leverage. An examination of the profit margin over this time shows an overall decline; battling the competition does have its costs, as does expansion. However, the profit margin has shown an increase lately.

Valuing the Company

The bottom of the Valuation Worksheet provides valuations using the earnings-based model. Applying the model to Toys "R" Us paints an interesting picture.

The first item that needs to be determined is the appropriate per share earnings figure for 1994. The worksheet uses an estimate based on the five-year earnings growth rate of 10.9% and the most recently reported earnings per share [1.65 x (1 + 0.109)], leading to a high valuation of $51.79 and a low valuation of $33.67. This compares to a current price of $34.62. Sounds enticing, but let's look at some of the assumptions.

Is the growth rate reasonable? Actually the growth rate used here (10.9%) is somewhat below the rates estimated by other analysts. For instance, Value Line estimates a higher growth rate of 17.5%, while the S&P Earnings Guide projects a growth rate of 18%. Using a higher growth rate would, of course, raise the valuations somewhat.

Of greater concern, however, are the high and low price-earnings ratios based on historical averages. These averages are based on a time period when the company was clearly a growth stock. But as we have seen, there are reasons to question whether the company can continue to be considered a growth firm.

If Toys "R" Us is valued as a mature stock, its price-earnings ratio would on average parallel the market's. Currently (mid-May 1994), the market's price-earnings ratio is 20.6; using that in the model would produce a valuation of $37.70 based on the worksheet's 1994 earnings per share estimate; using Value Line's higher 1994 earnings per share estimate would produce a valuation of around $41.

Conclusion

Examining different assumptions is a critical part of the valuation, and will help you isolate some of the major factors that are affecting a stock's price.

While the worksheet examines quantitative factors, it is clear that many subjective factors go into the equation. To judge these factors, it is necessary to go beyond the statistics. Any final decision should be based on a better understanding of the company, its management, and its competitive environment. This can only be accomplished by a thorough reading of the firm's financial reports, as well as the reports and summaries on the firm and its industry.

6

Investing in Utilities
for Income and Growth

Most investors look to utility stocks primarily for yield, with some expectation of share price increase. While utilities in the past have been viewed as staid, the industry is facing stiffer challenges from non-regulated sources, a tougher regulatory environment, and deregulation in certain areas.

Although growth prospects are limited, they do exist. Growth from a total return viewpoint—including both capital gains and dividends—usually emerges when a utility is positioned in an area with significant population growth, has deftly sidestepped the pitfalls of new plant construction, has diversified into non-regulated businesses that may prosper, or during potential takeover situations, which are increasingly common in the utility sector.

Company Characteristics

The average utility is still purchased for the dividend flow, which is usually two to three times the dividend yield of the average industrial stock. This yield component makes them competitive with bonds, and as such they are affected by changes in interest rates. In addition, the industry is highly leveraged, and interest costs consequently play a large role in the earnings equation. The combination of these two factors make utilities highly interest-rate sensitive: When interest rates fall, utilities rise in price, and when rates rise, utility prices suffer.

While the utility sector generally has lower risks, calamities do occur beyond the rare nuclear plant meltdown—construction delays and cost overruns, adverse regulatory decisions, failures in non-regulated businesses, unusual weather conditions affecting demand, and economic busts in single-industry dominated areas. Dividend cuts or suspensions on a stock bought primarily for dividend yield can be devastating.

Utility stocks are often recommended as defensive investments in times of economic uncertainty. The reasoning: If the economy turns down, the demand for electricity, gas, and water may decline somewhat for industrial users, but overall demand will not suffer significantly. Couple that with the likely decline in interest rates in an economic slowdown, and utility stocks can be expected to buck the trend of declining stock prices.

Conversely, interest rates tend to rise during expansions, and utility stocks tend to decline in this stage.

Many utilities offer dividend reinvestment programs, which provide investors with a low-transaction-cost method of reinvesting dividend payments; some plans also allow additional cash investments. The existence of a dividend reinvestment plan is an added investor benefit, but stock selection decisions should be based on fundamental merits.

The Initial List

For the beginning investor, there are several sources from which you can draw your initial list of promising utilities. Some suggestions are presented in Table 6-1. Most of these sources are inexpensive and may also be available in your local library. Keep in mind that these sources are useful primarily for the initial list. In addition, several are published annually, so the information may become dated. However, they do provide a starting point to narrow your search.

When searching for utilities, keep in mind that you are concentrating on an industry, but one that has several components: natural gas distributors, water companies, and electric utilities. Diversifying among these components—as well as geographically—would reduce some of the risks specific to the particular industry sector.

For most investors, utilities are primarily income plays. That means focusing not only on dividend yield, but also consistent dividend payments. A high ranking for earnings and dividends growth and stability, or a high rating for dividend safety by one of the information sources can narrow the selection.

Once a list of candidates is established, the next step is to perform an in-depth evaluation.

Table 6-1: Growth and Income Information Sources

Moody's Handbook of Dividend Achievers, annual edition—The book includes information on over 300 companies that have increased their dividends consistently over the past 10 years, many of which are utilities. The listings include a company's dividend achiever rank, as well as the company's dividend growth rate for the latest 10-year period. The book also provides full-page data summaries on each dividend achiever.

Standard & Poor's 500 Guide, annual edition
Standard & Poor's MidCap 400 Guide, annual edition
Standard & Poor's SmallCap 600 Guide, annual edition—These guides include this list: *Higher Dividends for Ten Years:* Firms that have paid higher cash dividends in each of the past 10 years and whose dividend yield is currently at least 2%, an indication of healthy finances and capable management. These annual guides include the full-page data pages found in the S&P's Stock Reports; since they are published annually, the data can be dated.

Standard & Poor's Industry Reports—Monthly review of 80 industries and some 900 stocks; utilities are divided into: electric utilities, natural gas and water suppliers. In the back of the industry reports are one-line listings for selected companies within each industry, allowing for comparison of the various firms listed relative to others in the same industry. For each stock, the S&P's earnings and dividend rank and S&P's evaluation of its investment potential (using their Stock Appreciation Ranking System) are included, which allow easy selection and comparison.   *Continued*

Table 6-1: Growth and Income Information Sources, *Cont'd*

Value Line Investment Survey—The tables in the back include several useful lists from which to draw prospects: *Conservative Stocks:* Stocks ranked high by value Line for relative safety. *High Yielding Stocks:* This consists almost entirely of utilities, ranked by yield, based on the projected dividends per share in three to five years, divided by recent price. *Widest Discount from Book Value and Lowest P/Es:* These lists may contain a smattering of utilities that may be good prospects.

Also of Note:
Standard & Poor's Industry Surveys—Provides major surveys on 21 industry groups annually that are updated periodically.

The following example is based on published information that was available in June of 1994 when the approach was applied.

SCANA Corp.: An Example

SCANA Corp. offers a good example of how the approach can be applied to utilities. In June of 1994, the firm appeared in Value Line's High-Yielding Stocks list (based on next year's estimated dividends per share) while at the same time ranking above average for relative safety. It also appeared in Moody's Handbook of Dividend Achievers, indicating it had increased its dividend consistently over the past 10 years. And it had a high S&P earnings and dividend ranking (A-) and was rated above average in appreciation potential by S&P (reported in Industry Reports).

SCANA Corp. is the holding company for South Carolina Electric & Gas Co., which provides electricity (74% of its revenues) and gas (26% of revenues) to central and southern South Carolina. Its fuels for generating electricity are coal (71%, according to Value Line), nuclear power (22%) and hydroelectric power (7%).

As with many utilities at the time, earnings growth projections were not stellar, due to little room for growth in its consumer base, and there were few uncertainties on the regulatory front. On the other hand, SCANA's expansion into non-regulated activities brings some promise to the earnings picture.

Figure 6-1 shows the completed valuation worksheet presented in the second chapter. Value Line was used as the source of both company and industry information.

A Tour of the Worksheet: Per Share Information

The first item that may strike you is that the May 31, 1994 stock price had fallen nearly 18% from its all-time high in 1993. This price drop reflected the overall decline that utilities faced due to rising interest rates at that time. On the other hand, SCANA's drop was much less than the industry's as a whole.

Next, it is important to examine the year-by-year earnings per share figures. Are they steadily increasing, or has there been a change in trend? SCANA earnings are only slowly increasing, except for 1992, when they dropped due primarily to increases in certain expenses. While 1993's earnings appear much higher, Value Line reports that earnings were inflated due to a particularly hot summer in which electricity demand was higher than usual. As a result, Value Line's projected earnings for 1994 are slightly below 1993 earnings, assuming normal weather conditions.

Dividends, on the other hand, increased only modestly every year. The five-year average growth rate is 2.7%, or slightly below the current rate of inflation.

In examining a utility, it is useful to compare the average growth rate in earnings relative to the average growth rate in dividends. This provides a measure of the potential stability and growth of the dividend, since over the long term, dividends cannot continue to grow faster than earnings. While both the growth rates for SCANA are modest, the

Figure 6-1: Valuation Worksheet

Company: SCANA Corp.   Current Price $ 43.88   Date (5 /31/ 94)

Ticker SCG   Exchange NYSE   Current P/E 11.6   Current Yield 6.4%

Financial Statement & Ratio Analysis

	Company						Industry or Competitor		Market
Per Share Information	19_89	19_90	19_91	19_92	19_93	5-year avg	19_93	5-year avg	19_93
Price: High	35.80	35.80	44.30	44.80	52.30				
Price: Low	29.60	30.30	33.50	38.60	40.10				
Earnings per Share (EPS)	3.04	3.31	3.37	2.84	3.72	growth rate: 5.2%			
Dividends per Share (DPS)	2.46	2.52	2.62	2.68	2.74	growth rate: 2.7%			
Book Value per Share (BV)	22.79	24.56	25.23	26.46	28.59				
Financial Ratios									
Price-Earnings Ratio (P/E): Avg	10.8	10.0	11.5	14.7	12.4	11.9	14.2	12.6*	21.3
High (High Price ÷ EPS)	11.8	10.8	13.1	15.8	14.1	13.1			
Low (Low Price ÷ EPS)	9.7	9.2	9.9	13.6	10.8	10.6			

Dividend Yield % (DY): Avg	7.6	7.6	6.9	6.4	6.0	6.9	5.5	6.3*	2.7
High (DPS ÷ Low Price)	8.3	8.3	7.8	6.9	6.8	7.6			
Low (DPS ÷ High Price)	6.9	7.0	5.9	6.0	5.2	6.2			
Payout Ratio % (DPS ÷ EPS)	80.9	76.1	77.7	94.4	73.3	80.5	79	82*	
Return on Equity % (EPS ÷ BV)	13.3	13.5	13.4	10.7	13.0	12.8	11.6	11.2*	
Financial Leverage %	49.8	46.2	50.1	49.2	50.2	49.1	49.0	49.9*	

*1990 through 1993

Valuation Estimates

Model based on earnings:

Average high P/E × estimated 19 _94_ EPS: _13.1_ × _3.60_ = _$47.16_ (high valuation estimate)
Average low P/E × estimated 19 _94_ EPS: _10.6_ × _3.60_ = _$38.16_ (low valuation estimate)

Model based on dividends:

Estimated 19 _94_ annual DPS ÷ average low DY: _2.82_ ÷ _0.062_ = _$45.48_ (high valuation estimate)
Estimated 19 _94_ annual DPS ÷ average high DY: _2.82_ ÷ _0.076_ = _$37.11_ (low valuation estimate)

Use decimal form for DY. For instance 5.4% would be 0.054.

five-year average earnings growth rate is above the
five-year average dividend growth rate.

Looking at the Financial Ratios

Dividend concerns tend to drive the prices of utility
stocks.

Not surprisingly, SCANA's dividend yield is
high at 6.4% compared to the market's June 1994
yield of 2.9%. However, it is not high relative to the
industry's 7% yield (for the Dow utility average),
and it is near its historical low of 6.2%. Higher than
average dividend yields are not necessarily an
indication of a good value (high dividends at a low
price); rather, they may indicate that the market
feels the dividend is in jeopardy.

The payout ratio (dividends per share divided
by earnings per share) also helps gauge the
strength of the dividend: The lower the payout
ratio, the better, implying that the dividend payment is more secure. A 100% payout ratio shows
that a firm is paying out all of its earnings to its
shareholders. The payout ratio for SCANA, 73.3%
in 1993, is near the industry average of 79%.

Financial leverage is another indication of dividend safety. Heavy debt loads saddle a company
with required cash outflows to bondholders, who
must be paid before dividends can be paid to
shareholders. Utilities tend to be heavily leveraged,
and interest costs have a major impact on a utility's
bottom line earnings. SCANA Corp.'s use of finan-

cial leverage, while high at 50.2% in 1993, is average for the industry, at 49% in 1993.

The 1993 return on equity of 13% for SCANA
Corp. was close to its long-term average and slightly above the industry's 11.6%. The return on equity
measures how well the firm is being run on both
an operational and financial basis. For regulated
utilities, return on equity is a function of the allow-
able rate of return, cost structure, and use of financial leverage. SCANA's use of financial leverage is
relatively unchanged. It appears that the firm has
instead been able to increase its competitive edge.

Valuing the Company

The bottom of the valuation worksheet provides
valuations using both the earnings-based model
and dividend-based model.

The first item that needs to be determined is the
appropriate per share earnings figure for 1994. The
worksheet uses the Value Line estimate of $3.60.
This produces a lower figure than an estimate
based on the five-year earnings growth rate of 5.2%
and the most recently reported earnings per share
of $3.72. The five-year growth rate is based on 1993
earnings that, according to Value Line, were high
due to extraordinary weather conditions; the Value
Line estimate for 1994 earnings per share is more
conservative, and in line with other analysts'
estimates as reported by S&P. Using the Value Line
estimates leads to a high valuation estimate of
$47.16 and a low valuation estimate of $38.16.

Determining the appropriate dividends per share figure for 1994 is somewhat easier. Using the five-year growth rate to project next year's dividend produces a $2.81 estimate [$2.74 x (1 + 0.027)], almost identical to Value Line's projection of $2.82.

Using the Value Line figure in the dividend model produces a high valuation estimate of $45.48 and a low valuation estimate of $37.11.

The May 31, 1994 price of SCANA Corp. was $43.88, which falls in between the two valuations—neither a screaming buy, nor an obvious sell. But remember, this is a utility.

SCANA offers a dividend reinvestment plan, and allows investors to buy initial shares directly from the firm.

Conclusion

The current level of the dividend, the expected growth and the safety of the dividend payment, and the overall interest rate environment drive the prices of utility stocks. Examining these features is critical in your evaluation. The valuation models will most likely not turn up any startling results. But remember—what you are looking for is high income with some growth potential, at a fair price.

While the worksheet examines quantitative factors, it is clear that many subjective factors go into the equation. To judge these factors, it is necessary to go beyond the statistics. Any final decision should be based on a better understanding of the company, its management, and its competitive and regulatory environment. Table 6-2 provides a summary of these factors. However, a full understanding can only be accomplished by a thorough reading of the firm's financial reports, as well as the reports and summaries on the firm and its industry.

Table 6-2: Some Factors to Consider When Evaluating a Utility

Company Factors	Questions to ask:
Type of Unitility Electric Gas Water	Is the utility diversified or of one particular type? Diversification among various types of utilities helps reduce some of the risks of investing in this sector. Are there changes in the competitive or regulatory environment that may affect a particular type of utility?
Customer Base Residential Commercial Industrial	Does any one predominate? Is the population growing, with the potential for an expanding residential base? Are there external factors (for instance, extraordinary weather conditions, or an eco- nomic downturn) that may affect industrial or commercial use?
Power Source Nuclear Coal Gas Oil Hydroelectric	Does any source of power predominate? What factors affect the cost of the power sources? Items to look for include the age of a nuclear plant; type of coal used and where it is obtained; the priceand supply of oil; weather patterns that may affect hydroelectric power.

Other Factors	
Non-regulated businesses	Is the utility moving into non-regulated businesses, and if so, how risky and how promising are they? Is there potential for reducing operating costs by better management and/or new technology?
Management	
Technology	

External Factors

Economic	
Interest rate outlook	What is the outlook for interest rates? Rising rates affect the cost of borrowing, a major cost to a utility. What stage in the business cycle is the economy? A sagging economy can affect industrial and commercial use.
Business Cycle	
Regulatory	What laws and regulations may affect the industry? On the national level, federal laws concerning the environment may affect some utilities more than others. At the state level, where utility rates are controlled, what is the regulatory mood?
Federal	
State	

7

A Strategy for Investing in Undervalued Stocks

A strategy that focuses on low price-earnings ratios is a value approach that can help you find stocks with hidden or undiscovered potential for significant price appreciation, provided you are correct in your assessment of the firm and the market eventually comes to agree with you. This strategy can produce more income in the form of dividends than other strategies, and it tends to be less volatile; on the other hand, it requires patience, since it can take time for the market to recognize value.

Stock Characteristics

Value investors are searching for undervalued companies—firms whose stocks are selling at prices below their true per-share "worth." How do you measure worth? One measure focuses on the amount of earnings that will be generated by the firm in the future on each share of stock.

A stock's price-earnings ratio—its share price divided by the most recent 12-months' earnings per share—embodies the market's expectations of a company's ability to generate earnings. If the market has low earnings growth expectations for the firm or it views earnings as uncertain, it will not be willing to pay as much per share as it would for a firm with high earnings growth expectations. The share price on these firms is bid down, and the result is a low price-earnings ratio.

That doesn't mean that all stocks with low price-earnings ratios have little or no growth potential. While many do, indeed, deserve their low ratios, value investors hope to identify firms that the market has misjudged—firms that really do have potential and whose stocks are undervalued either out of neglect or due to a market overreaction to bad news.

Stocks that have low price-earnings ratios may be in out-of-favor industries, or in cyclical industries that are close to their down phase. In addition, they may have other traits indicating their out-of-favor status, including high dividend yields (if the firm pays dividends) and low price-to-book-value ratios (book value per share is total assets less all liabilities divided by shares outstanding, and is a measure of the firm's net worth per share).

These stocks also tend to be less volatile, since bad news is already reflected in their relatively low prices. On the other hand, it may take considerable time for the market to recognize value, and of course, there is the risk that the market was right in its assessment after all.

The Initial List

Suggested sources from which you can draw your initial list of potential undervalued stocks are presented in Table 7-1. Many may be available in your local library.

The initial lists suggested here for beginners include not only lists of stocks with low price-earnings ratios, but also lists of stocks with other indications of undervaluation, for example low price-to-book-value. Certain industries will dominate any list of stocks ranked only by price-earnings ratio. In addition, focusing only on stocks with the lowest ratios may turn up a list of stocks with no growth potential. Using other qualifying screens and indications of undervaluation will expand your universe of potential value plays, and will help ensure that you do not accidentally concentrate too much on one specific industry.

Cyclical firms are likely to appear on many lists, so it would be useful to examine earnings growth over time periods covering at least one economic cycle to make sure you are focusing on long-term earnings trends. In addition, firms with years of negative earnings are likely to turn up. Negative earnings per share produce meaningless price-earnings ratios, and it can be difficult to form a judgment concerning a stock's average price- earnings ratio if there are several years with meaningless numbers. Examining a firm's price-earnings ratio over a much longer time period—perhaps even 10 years—may help. The trade-off, however, is that the company may have changed fundamentally over this time.

Table 7-1: Undervalued Stock Source List

Standard & Poor's Earnings Guide—Includes summary information and focuses on earnings and earnings growth estimates. The front includes short useful lists, some of which appear periodically. *Strong EPS & Dividends to P/E Ratio:* This is a value measure that compares earnings growth (earnings growth and the dividend yield) to the price earnings ratio. Inclusion is limited to firms that pay dividends and have five years of positive earnings. *Potential Value Plays:* These firms are selling at a discount to net tangible book value, a maximum price-earnings ratio (based on next year's earnings estimates) of 15 and a projected 10% increase in earnings. *Low Rank, Low Price, Estimates Up:* These firms have low rankings, indicating a history of disappointing earnings and dividend payments, and all suffered losses in the last year. However, they are expected to be profitable this year and show strong earnings gains by next year. *Forward Growth and Low P/Es:* These firms are selling at price-earnings ratios of less than 12 based on future estimates, but earnings are expected to increase at least 10% over the next five years. *Bargains Based on Earnings Prospects:* This lists stocks with low price-earnings ratios relative to their projected five-year earnings growth rates.

Continued

Table 7-1: Undervalued Stock Source List, *Cont'd*

Value Line Investment Survey—Part I Summary & Index: The tables in the back include these useful lists: *Widest Discounts from Book Value:* This consists of stocks whose ratios of recent price to book value are the lowest. *Lowest P/Es:* This consists of stocks whose current price-earnings ratios based on estimated earnings are the lowest. *Bargain Basement Stocks:* These firms have low price-earnings ratios as well as price-to-net-working-capital (current assets less all liabilities) ratios that are in the bottom quartile of Value Line stocks.

Standard & Poor's Industry Reports—This is a monthly review of 80 industries and some 900 stocks. In the back of the industry reports are one-line listings for the selected companies within each industry, allowing for comparison of the various firms listed relative to others in the same industry. For each stock, the S&P's earnings and dividend rank, and S&P's evaluation of its investment potential (using their Stock Appreciation Ranking System) is included, which allows easy selection and comparison.

Lastly, keep in mind that this is a contrarian strategy. The written analyses about the firms or industries that appear in these lists may not be particularly enthusiastic and many may be quite negative. It is important to understand why most analysts hold the views they do, and most often they are correct. It may take some digging combined with independent judgment on your part to find potentially undervalued firms.

Once a potential stock is spotted, the next step is an in-depth evaluation to determine the fair market value.

Chrysler Corp.: An Example

Chrysler Corp. offers a good example of the low price-earnings ratio approach to valuation. In July of 1994, appeared in the Value Line list of stocks with the lowest price-earnings ratios; Ford and GM also appear on the list, although Chrysler is the lowest. It had a low earnings and dividend ranking (B-) from Standard & Poor's, but was rated in the highest category for appreciation potential by Standard & Poor's (reported in S&P's Industry Reports).

Chrysler is the third largest automobile and truck manufacturer in the U.S. It is in a cyclical industry that was hurt badly by the 1990-91 recession but then staged a strong turnaround during 1993. According to Value Line, the firm in early 1994 had strong sales, and in fact was at peak capacity for most of its vehicles.

Figure 7-1 shows the completed valuation worksheet presented in Chapter 2. Value Line was used as the source of both company and industry information.

Entering the per share data from an information source is relatively straightforward, but it is important to stick to the same source for company information, since reporting services make different adjustments to the data they provide. Value Line is used for the data here, and the earnings figures include non-recurring gains and losses.

A Tour of the Worksheet: Per Share Information

The first item of note is the price. During 1993 the stock was at its five-year high.

The year-by-year earnings per share figures indicate how badly the firm fared during the early 1990s. Clearly earnings were increasing by 1994, but the five-year growth rate figure of 49% is unsustainable over the long term; earnings had increased, but were unlikely to continue at the same pace. Value Line projected earnings in 1994 to be up substantially, at $8.00 per share, an 18% increase over 1993.

Dividends were halved in 1991, but were increased slightly in 1993 and again in 1994. With the recovery in earnings, it was unlikely that dividends would drop further; using the five-year average dividend growth rate figure of -14% to project next year's dividends is misleading. The 1994 annual indicated dividend was $1.00.

Figure 7-1: Valuation Worksheet

Company: Chrysler

Ticker: C   Exchange NYSE   Current Price $ 47.50   Current P/E 6.2   Current Yield 2.1%   Date (6 /30/ 94)

Financial Statement & Ratio Analysis

	Company						Industry or Competitor		Market
	19 89	19 90	19 91	19 92	19 93	5-year avg	19 93	5-year avg	19 93
Per Share Information									
Price: High	29.60	20.40	15.90	33.90	58.40				
Price: Low	18.10	9.10	9.80	11.50	31.80				
Earnings per Share (EPS)	1.36	0.30	−2.74	1.38	6.77	growth rate: 49%			
Dividends per Share (DPS)	1.20	1.20	0.60	0.60	0.65	growth rate: −14%			
Book Value per Share (BV)	32.42	30.53	20.91	25.47	19.32				
Financial Ratios									
Price-Earnings Ratio (P/E): Avg	17.5	49.2	NMF	16.4	6.7	22.5*	11.5	NMF	21.3
High (High Price ÷ EPS)	21.8	68.0	NMF	24.6	8.6	30.7*			
Low (Low Price ÷ EPS)	13.3	30.3	NMF	8.3	4.7	14.2*			

Dividend Yield % (DY): Avg	5.3	9.5	4.9	3.5	1.5	4.9	2.2	4.5**	2.7
High (DPS ÷ Low Price)	6.6	13.2	6.1	5.2	2.0	6.6			
Low (DPS ÷ High Price)	4.1	5.9	3.8	1.8	1.1	3.3			
Payout Ratio % (DPS ÷ EPS)	88.2	400	-21.9	43.5	9.6	135.2*	33.0	NMF	
Return on Equity % (EPS ÷ BV)	4.2	1.0	NMF	5.4	35.0	11.4*	25.4	NMF	
Financial Leverage %	235	186	245	178	100	189	327	259**	

*An average of 4 years, which excludes 1991.

**1990 through 1993.

NMF: no meaningful figure

Valuation Estimates

Model based on earnings:

Average high P/E × estimated 19 94 EPS: 30.7 × $8.00 = $245.60 (high valuation estimate)

Average low P/E × estimated 19 94 EPS: 14.2 × $8.00 = $113.60 (low valuation estimate)

Model based on dividends:

Estimated 19 94 annual DPS ÷ average low DY: $1.00 ÷ 0.033 = $30.30 (high valuation estimate)

Estimated 19 94 annual DPS ÷ average high DY: $1.00 ÷ 0.066 = $15.15 (low valuation estimate)

Use decimal form for DY. For instance 5.4% would be 0.054.

Looking at the Financial Ratios

Earnings concerns appeared to be driving the price of Chrysler stock.

The price-earnings ratio of Chrysler appeared at a considerable low, relative to its five-year historical norms. However, most of these price-earnings levels were produced at a time of extremely poor earnings for Chrysler. In 1990, for instance, Chrysler had earnings per share of only $0.30. The extraordinarily high price-earnings multiple in 1990 of 68.0 is due in large part to this extraordinarily low earnings per share level, and not due to high expectations for growth. Its July 1994 price-earnings ratio of 6.2, however, was slightly below its average for 1993.

Chrysler's dividend yield paints a somewhat different picture. It had dropped substantially from its 1990 high of 9.5%. High dividend yields can indicate a good value (high dividends at a low price), or they may indicate that the market feels the dividend is in jeopardy—a feeling that was justified by the dividend cut in 1991. Dividend yields are most useful as indicators of value when dividends have held steady, and in Chrysler's case they had not. The July 1994 dividend yield of 2.1% was still below the level reached after the dividend cut, but above its 1993 high.

The payout ratio (dividends per share divided by earnings per share) helps gauge the strength of the dividend: The lower the payout ratio, the better, implying that the dividend payment is more secure.

A 100% payout ratio shows that a firm is paying out all of its earnings to its shareholders. The payout ratio for Chrysler had ranged all over the board, but indicated that the dividend is not in jeopardy.

The 1993 return on equity for Chrysler Corp. was above the industry average. Again, however, the historical figures are difficult to interpret. The return on equity measures how well the firm is being run on both an operational and financial basis. To boost return on equity, a company must increase the profit margin on goods being sold, make better use of its assets, or increase the level of financial leverage. Chrysler's use of financial leverage, however, had been decreasing—and was below the industry norm. While times were good, Chrysler had been reducing its debt.

Valuing the Company

The bottom of the Valuation Worksheet provides valuations using both the earnings-based model and dividend-based models.

The first item that needs to be determined is the appropriate per share earnings figure for 1994. The worksheet uses the more conservative Value Line estimate of $8.00 rather than a figure based on historical growth, since the five-year earnings growth rate is misleading.

Another problem is the average price-earnings ratio figure. The figure used on the worksheet uses four years (1991 is excluded because the negative earnings per share figure for that year produces meaningless figures). This produces a high valuation estimate of $245.60 and a low valuation estimate of $113.60. The price-earnings ratio in 1990 of 49.2, however, was extraordinarily high, due to the extremely low earnings per share figure that year. Excluding this year from the estimates, and using price-earnings ratios from only three years, would produce a high valuation of $146.40 and a low valuation of $70.40.

An even better approach, however, would be to examine the price-earnings ratio over a much longer time period—for instance, 10 years. This time period covers a complete economic cycle, and would provide a more appropriate price-earnings range. Using these figures (but still excluding 1990) provides a high valuation of $79.76 and a low valuation of $40.47.

Chrysler's July 1994 price of $47.50 was in the low range even using the 10-year averages, but it was not the obvious buy that it appeared at first blush using the five-year figures.

The 1994 indicated dividend of $1.00 per share is used in the dividend valuation model. The dividend model produces a high valuation of $30.30 and a low valuation of $15.15, based on the five-year high and low dividend yield averages. Ten-year dividend yield averages would produce a high valuation of $33.89 and a low valuation of $18.16. Chrysler clearly appeared overvalued based on the dividend yield model.

Which model is more appropriate? The stock in July 1994 was priced considerably above the valuations based on the dividend yield model. It is far more likely that earnings expectations, rather than dividend considerations, are driving the price of the stock.

The earnings models produced a wide range of valuations. Which one is most useful? Valuations based on earnings can be problematic for cyclical stocks, particularly if they are at their high points. The valuations based on the 10-year historical ratios are probably the most appropriate. An even more conservative approach would be to use the 10-year average *low* price-earnings ratio as the norm, and to purchase the stock only if it falls below the valuation based on that ratio. Using an average of its earnings per share over the last five years instead of 1994 estimated earnings per share would also be more conservative. Using either of these as a guide, Chrysler in July of 1994 would appear to be overvalued, or at least fairly valued.

Conclusion

While the worksheet examines quantitative factors, it is clear that many subjective factors go into the equation. Any final decision should be based on a better understanding of the company, its management, and its competitive environment.

8

Using Analysts' Estimates
To Your Advantage

When purchasing a stock, an investor must first form an expectation concerning the outlook for the company and the stock's price. But stock prices are driven by market expectations—the overall expectations of all investors—and stock prices change as the market's expectations change.

Tracking those expectations can provide some clues to the future direction of a stock's price. This can be done by examining the earnings estimates made by analysts at major investment research firms who follow the stock.

This chapter focuses on a basic approach that takes advantage of changes in expectations to turn up promising candidates.

In using earnings estimates, the first rule to keep in mind is that the current price usually reflects the consensus earnings estimate. It is common to see price declines for stocks that report earnings increases from the previous reporting period because in many cases, while the actual earnings represent an increase, the increase is not as great as the market had expected. Earnings surprises occur when a company reports actual earnings that differ from consensus earnings estimates.

During the earnings reporting season, financial newspapers such as the *Wall Street Journal* provide daily reports on earnings announcements. Firms with significant earnings surprises are often highlighted.

Positive earnings surprises occur when actual reported earnings are significantly above the forecasted earnings per share. Negative earnings surprises occur when reported earnings per share are significantly below the earnings expectations. The stock prices of firms with significant positive earnings surprises show above average performance, while those with negative surprises have below average performance.

Changes in stock price resulting from an earnings surprise can be felt immediately, and the surprise also has a long-term effect. Studies indicate that the effect can persist for as long as a year after the announcement. This means that it does not make sense to buy a stock after the initial price decline of a negative earnings surprise. There is a good chance that the stock will continue to underperform the market for some time. It also indicates that it may not be too late to buy into an attractive company after a better than expected earnings report is released.

Not surprisingly, large firms tend to adjust to surprises more quickly than small firms. Larger firms are tracked by more analysts and portfolio managers, who tend to act quickly.

Firms with a significant quarterly earnings surprise also often have earnings surprises in subsequent quarters. When a firm has a surprise, it often is a sign that other similar surprises will follow. This is sometimes referred to as the cockroach effect—like cockroaches, you rarely see just one earnings surprise.

Revisions to earnings estimates lead to price adjustments similar to earnings surprises. When earnings estimates are revised significantly upward—5% or more—stocks tend to show above average performance. Stock prices of firms with downward revisions show below average performance.

Changes in estimates reflect changes in expectations of future performance. Perhaps the economic outlook is better than previously expected, or maybe a new product is selling better than anticipated.

Revisions are often precursors to earnings surprises. As the reporting period approaches, estimates normally converge toward the consensus. A flurry of revisions near the reporting period can indicate that analysts missed the mark and are scrambling to improve their estimates.

Table 8-1 summarizes the main points to keep in mind when dealing with consensus earnings estimates.

Stock Characteristics

Research on earnings estimates indicates that investing in stocks of companies with significant upward revisions in analysts' earnings estimates and positive earnings surprises leads to above-average returns.

Table 8-1: Using Consensus Earnings Estimates

Earnings Estimates: Firms with high expected earnings growth tend to underperform the market because it is difficult to meet the market's high expectations. Companies with low earnings expectations tend to do better than expected.

Prices embody current earnings estimates.

Earnings Estimate Revisions: Stock prices of firms with significant upward revisions (5% or more) generally outperform the market. Firms with significant downward revisions underperform the market. Earnings revisions are often a precursor to earnings surprises. Stock prices react positively to upward revisions.

Earnings Surprise: Stock prices of firms that significantly exceed their earnings expectations (positive earnings surprise) outperform the market, while those with negative earnings surprises underperform.

The earnings surprise effect is long-lasting. The greatest effect of the surprise can be felt immediately, but the effect of the earnings surprise can be seen for as long as a year. The effect of the surprise tends to be longer lasting for negative earnings surprises. The stock prices of large firms adjust to surprises more quickly than those of small firms. Earnings surprises often follow in groups—the cockroach effect.

The chance of an earnings surprise is greater if the range of estimates for a company is wide.

The price move can be more dramatic, however, if an earnings surprise occurs for a firm with a very tight range of earnings estimates.

If any general company characteristics can be associated with stocks that have earnings surprises, it is that they are in a state of change and uncertainty. The environment of uncertainty may come out of an overall economic change, such as an economy on the verge of a turnaround. A change within an industry, such as the unanticipated impact of a new regulation, or even a change within an individual company, such as the use of new technology, may also cause uncertainty.

The Initial List

Suggested sources from which you can draw your initial list are presented in Table 8-2 and in Appendix A at the back of the book. Many may be available in your local library.

Earnings estimates can be used in a variety of ways. For the purpose of spotting promising candidates, you would want to concentrate on those firms that would benefit from changes in expectations. That would mean looking for these characteristics:

• Stocks of firms with significant positive revisions in the earnings expectations of analysts.
• Stocks of firms whose recent earnings reports significantly exceeded earnings expectations (a positive earnings surprise).

Table 8-2: Sources of Information
for the Initial List

Analyst Watch—Reports earnings estimates from analysts for over 4,000 stocks. Includes a section near the front called Criteria Screens, which has a large number of listings based on earnings estimates, including largest positive earnings revisions covering various periods and best earnings surprises.

Institutional Brokers' Estimate System (I/B/E/S)
Monthly Summary Data Book—Reports earnings estimates from analysts for over 4,000 stocks. The Highlights section provides a number of useful lists, including the 40 largest estimate increases over the previous month, and companies with the largest positive quarterly earnings surprises.

Nelson's Earnings Outlook—Reports earnings estimates from analysts on 3,000 stocks. The front includes listings that indicate the most significant estimate changes (both up and down) over the last 30, 90, and 180 days.

Standard & Poor's Earnings Guide—Includes summary (one-line) information and focuses on earnings and earnings growth estimates from analysts. The front includes this useful list: *Significant 1994 Estimate Changes:* These are firms that have had significant changes in 1994 earnings estimates from analysts since the previous month.

Continued

Table 8-2: Sources of Information for the Initial List, *Cont'd*

Two other lists appear periodically in the **Standard & Poor's Earnings Guide** that may also be useful: *Substantial Estimate and Price Increases from Year-End:* These are firms whose earnings estimates have increased by at least 20% and whose stock prices have gone up by at least 20%. *Tight Earnings Projections:* These are firms in which analysts' high and low estimates don't differ more than 10%. Given the tight range of estimates, any earnings ``surprises'' would have a large impact on these stocks.

Value Line Investment Survey—Value Line provides its own earnings estimates for companies it covers. It does not have a separate list of companies with earnings revisions. However, the Summary has one-line listings for all companies, and indicates earnings revisions with an arrow next to the estimate. The tables in the back (see index for the page numbers) also includes this list: *Stocks Moving Up In Rank:* This consists of stocks of firms who have moved up in Value Line's Timeless ranks, primarily those caused by new earnings reports where earnings were higher than expected.

- Stocks of firms with a tight range of earnings estimates, where a positive earnings surprise would have the largest impact, or stocks of firms with a wide range of earnings estimates where a positive earnings surprise would be most likely.

Make sure that the list you are using is recent. Also keep in mind that the stocks selected under this approach are likely to receive a fair amount of coverage, making the likelihood of uncovering "hidden potential" unlikely. Only if you disagree with the consensus, and feel earnings will once again come in higher than expected, will there be the potential for above-average returns.

Once a potential stock is spotted, the next step is an in-depth evaluation to determine the fair market value. The following example is based on published information that was available in August of 1994, when the approach was applied.

NACCO Industries: An Example

NACCO Industries offers a good example of this approach. It was chosen because it appeared in *S&P's Earnings Guide* in its list of Significant 1994 Estimate Changes, and in the Value Line Summary where an upward earnings revision was indicated in the summary listings.

NACCO Industries is classified in the machinery (construction and mining) industry, a cyclical industry. However, it is actually a holding company with three subsidiaries: a forklift manufacturing group (Hyster-Yale); a small appliance manufacturer (Hamilton Beach/Proctor-Silex); and a coal mining firm (North American Coal Corp.).

The industry as a whole, according to Value Line, had posted earnings above those that were expected due to better than expected sales both domestically and abroad.

In line with this, NACCO's forklift manufacturing subsidiary had a large second quarter sales increase. Lower manufacturing costs also helped its other subsidiary, Hamilton Beach, in the second quarter.

According to Value Line, the biggest concern was how soon this cyclical industry boom would peak and begin to drop off.

Figure 8-1 shows the completed valuation worksheet introduced in Chapter 2. Value Line was used as the source of both company and industry information.

A Tour of the Worksheet: Per Share Information

The first item of note is the August 1994 price, which was near its high for 1993. The price had stayed within a wide range since 1990, and had not since risen above the top of this range.

At the same time, year-by-year earnings per share showed a fairly sharp drop over the years, from $5.26 in 1989 to only $1.30 in 1993, leading to a five-year growth rate of -29.5%. However, NACCO is a cyclical firm, and earnings in mid-1994 were heading up, not down. For that reason, the five-year earnings growth rate is not particularly

Figure 8-1: Valuation Worksheet

Company: NACCO Industries 'A'   Current Price $ 58.00   Date (8 /12/ 94)

Ticker NC   Exchange NYSE   Current P/E 21.8   Current Yield 1.2%

Financial Statement & Ratio Analysis

	Company						Industry or Competitor		Market
Per Share Information	19_89	19_90	19_91	19_92	19_93	5-year avg	19_93	5-year avg	19_93
Price: High	56.00	70.50	56.90	60.00	58.30				
Price: Low	31.30	22.00	29.00	34.30	42.00				
Earnings per Share (EPS)	5.26	4.87	2.31	2.71	1.30	growth rate: -29.5%			
Dividends per Share (DPS)	0.58	0.60	0.62	0.64	0.66	growth rate: 3.3%			
Book Value per Share (BV)	33.89	39.75	39.44	26.82	26.35				
Financial Ratios									
Price-Earnings Ratio (P/E): Avg	8.3	9.5	18.6	17.4	38.6	18.4	16.6	**	21.3
High (High Price ÷ EPS)	10.6	14.5	24.6	22.1	44.8	23.0			
Low (Low Price ÷ EPS)	6.0	4.5	12.6	12.7	32.3	13.9			

Dividend Yield % (DY): Avg	1.4	1.8	1.6	1.5	1.4	1.5	1.8	**	2.7
High (DPS ÷ Low Price)	1.9	2.7	2.1	1.9	1.6	2.0			
Low (DPS ÷ High Price)	1.0	0.9	1.1	1.1	1.1	1.0			
Payout Ratio % (DPS ÷ EPS)	11.0	12.3	26.8	23.6	50.8	24.4	30	**	
Return on Equity % (EPS ÷ BV)	15.5	12.3	5.9	10.1	4.9	10.7	14.8	6.2***	
Financial Leverage* %	240	234	213	192	152	206	80	68***	

*Long-term debt ÷ equity   **Not enough years with meaningful stats   ***1990 through 1993

Valuation Estimates

Model based on earnings:

Average high P/E × estimated 19 94 EPS: 23.0 × 4.35 = $100.05 using 4-yr P/E: $78.30 (high)
Average low P/E × estimated 19 94 EPS: 13.9 × 4.35 = $60.46 using 4-yr P/E: $39.15 (low)

Model based on dividends:

Estimated 19 94 annual DPS ÷ average low DY: 0.68 ÷ 0.01 = $68.00 (high valuation estimate)
Estimated 19 94 annual DPS ÷ average high DY: 0.68 ÷ 0.02 = $34.00 (low valuation estimate)

Use decimal form for DY. For instance 5.4% would be 0.054.

useful in projecting next year's earnings. The Value Line earnings estimate for 1994 was $4.35, an increase of 234% over 1993 earnings.

Dividends remained fairly steady over the prior five years, with a five-year growth rate of only 3.3%. Value Line's estimate of $0.68 shows a continuation of that modest increase.

Looking at the Financial Ratios

The price-earnings ratio of NACCO, at 21.8 in mid-August 1994, was close to its five-year average high, and below its lowest level in 1993. However, the 1993 price-earnings range of 32.3 to 44.8 was extremely high due in large part to the cyclically low earnings per share level, and not due to high expectations for growth. The abnormally high 1993 figures tend to distort the five-year average; a four-year average, excluding 1993, produces an average price-earnings ratio of 13.5, with a four-year average high of 18.0 and a four-year average low of 9.0. The August 1994 price-earnings ratio was above these four-year averages, in line with expectations at that time regarding earnings growth.

NACCO's dividend yield of 1.2% in August of 1994 was close to its five-year low. Dividend yields (dividends per share divided by price) are most useful as indicators of value when dividends have been significant and steady, which they have been. Normally, a low dividend yield relative to the historical level indicates a relatively high market valuation for the firm, if dividend considerations are a driving force behind the stock price.

NACCO's payout ratio in 1993 almost doubled, due to its abnormally low earnings per share figure for that year. A firm's payout ratio (dividends per share divided by earnings per share) helps gauge the strength of the dividend by indicating how much of a firm's earnings are paid out to shareholders. The lower the payout ratio, the better, implying dividend payments are more secure. Excluding 1993, NACCO's payout ratio had been low, indicating that the dividend was not in jeopardy. Earnings per share were expected to increase much more than dividends, so NACCO's payout ratio would likely drop back to pre-1993 levels.

The 1993 return on equity of 4.9% was below the industry average of 14.8%, although the abnormally low 1993 earnings per share figure distorts that year's return on equity figure. Return on equity measures how well the firm is managed both operationally and financially. To boost return on equity, a company must increase its profits from sales, manufacture its goods more efficiently, or increase the level of financial leverage. NACCO's use of financial leverage had been steadily decreasing, but it was above the industry norm. One would expect to see a return on equity higher than the industry average with above-average financial leverage.

Valuing the Company

The bottom of the Valuation Worksheet provides valuations using both the earnings-based model and dividend-based models.

For the earnings-based models, the 1994 earnings per share figure used is the Value Line projection, since a projection based on the five-year average growth rate would be misleading. For the dividend-based models, the dividends per share figure is based on the five-year average growth rate, which matches the Value Line projection.

The five-year averages for the high and low price-earnings ratios and high and low dividend yields were also used in the worksheet. The results: The earnings-based models produced a valuation range of $60.46 to $100.05, while the dividend-based models produced a range of $34.00 to $68.00.

The valuations produced by the earnings model would indicate that the stock in August of 1994 was underpriced at a time when earnings expectations were clearly rising—an unlikely occurrence. That is a reason to question the assumptions used in the model.

As we noted earlier, the five-year average price-earnings ratio figures are distorted by the abnormally high ratios in 1993. A four-year average that excludes 1993 would be more appropriate. Using the four-year average in the earnings-based model produces a valuation range of $39.15 to $78.30.

What about the dividend-based model? Since dividend considerations do not appear to be much of a factor affecting NACCO's price, this model is not useful here.

NACCO's price currently in August of 1994 was about $58.00, close to midpoint between the four-year high and four-year low earnings-based valuations. That indicates a fairly priced stock.

If you agree with the consensus outlook for earnings, as indicated by the Value Line estimates, don't expect to be rewarded by above-average returns. However, if you expect that earnings per share will come in higher than expected by the consensus, there will be a potential for another earnings surprise—and the potential for above-average returns.

Conclusion

A careful examination of the assumptions is a critical part of the valuation, and will help you identify factors that could be misleading.

While the worksheet examines quantitative factors, it is clear that many subjective factors go into the equation. Any final decision should be based on a better understanding of the company, its management, and its competitive environment. This can only be accomplished by a thorough reading of the firm's financial reports, as well as the reports and summaries on the firm and its industry.

9

A Basic Approach to Finding Stocks With Winning Characteristics

One way to develop a strategy is to base it on what has worked in the past. With that in mind, one study examined the characteristics of a group of winning stocks. The goal was to try to find common traits that could be used to develop trading rules for identifying potential winners.

Applying the rules in a series of stock screens, of course, requires a computer. Can the trading rules be adapted to a basic strategy for beginners?

This chapter focuses on a basic approach that looks for stocks with some of the major characteristics of stock market winners.

Winning Characteristics

In the original study, nine characteristics of winning stocks were found. However, several characteristics were related, and they can be broken down into four common attributes:

1. A price-to-book value ratio less than 1.0. Book value is total assets less all debt. A price-to-book-value ratio below 1.0 indicates the share price of the firm is below the net assets of the firm—an indication that it may be undervalued.

2. Accelerating earnings. An indication that the firm may be starting to turn around.

3. High and increasing relative strength. Relative strength is a technical indicator of the price change of the stock relative to the price changes of other stocks. Stocks with strong recent relative strength are considered likely to continue their performance—in other words, they have momentum that is greater than the market's movement.

4. Fewer than 20 million common shares outstanding. This characteristic eliminates the very large firms. Stocks with a lesser number of shares outstanding are considered more likely to have stronger price performance once the market "discovers" the stock and starts to bid up share price, since there is less liquidity.

An approach based on these characteristics is looking for stocks that are out-of-favor and neglected (low price-to-book value), are starting to turn around financially (accelerating earnings), are just starting to be recognized by the market (high and rising relative strength), and are likely to register strong price appreciation (lower number of shares outstanding).

The Initial List

A big hurdle in applying this approach is developing your initial list. That's because you are looking for stocks that fit several criteria. There are lists of stocks that meet the rules individually, but it would be rare to find a stock that appeared on each list.

The easiest approach is to start with a list of stocks that meet one rule—low price-to-book-value ratios, for instance. Then glance over the full-page reports (in a source such as Value Line Investment Survey) of each of the stocks in the first list, looking to see if any of those stocks fulfill the other requirements.

Lists of firms with low price-to-book value ratios are suggested as the starting point because book value screens can be harder to find. Only a relatively small number of financially strong firms will be selling for prices that are below book value. Relative strength can also be difficult to find, so restricting your initial search to sources that provide at least one of these two figures will save you some time. However, more firms will have high relative strength (above 70% in the *Investor's Business Daily* listing) than will pass the book value screen.

Information on accelerating earnings and number of shares outstanding are available from sources that provide full-page data listings on individual stocks (such as Value Line and S&P).

Suggested sources from which you can draw your initital list are presented in Table 9-1 above and in Appenidix A at the back of the book. Many may be available in your local public library.

Once a potential stock is spotted, the next step is an in-depth evaluation to determine the fair market value.

Table 9-1: "Winners" Information Sources

Lists of Stocks With Low Price-to-Book Values:

Standard & Poor's Earnings Guide—Includes summary (one-line) information and focuses on earnings and earnings growth estimates; note that these one-line summaries do not include book value. However, the front includes one short useful list: *Potential Value Plays:* These firms are selling at a discount to net tangible book value, a maximum price-earnings ratio (based on next year's earnings estimates) of 15 and a projected 10% increase in earnings.

Value Line Investment Survey—Part I Summary & Index: The tables in the back (see index for the page numbers) include this useful list: *Widest Discount from Book Value:* This consists of stocks whose ratios of recent price to book value are the lowest.

Relative Strength Figures:

Investor's Business Daily—Realtive strength and other momentum indicators are listed for every stock in the daily stock listsgs. (Price-earnings ratios, a measure of undervaluation that can be a proxy for low price-to-book-value ratios, are listed for every stock each Wednesday).

Value Line Investment Survey—The one-page descriptions of each stock include a graphical depiction of a stock's relative strength, so you can tell by glancing at the graph whether it is high or rising.

Contitnued

Table 9-1: "Winners" Information Sources, *Cont'd*

Corporate Financial Data (including book value, quarterly earnings and number of shares:

Standard & Poor's Stock Reports—Company reports are found in volumes according to the exchange on which they are traded; presents 10 years of data.

Value Line Investment Survey—Analyses over 1,600 common stocks; presents 15 years of data.

The following example is based on published information that was available in September of 1994, when the approach was applied.

Moog Inc.: An Example

Moog Inc. offers a good example of a firm that meets the restrictions of this approach. The first step was to look at a list of companies that were selling for below book value. Then, each of those stocks was examined using the full-page listings in the Value Line Investment Survey.

Moog passed the first test here, which was to have a high and rising relative strength. The quarterly earnings box was then examined to see if quarterly earnings were trending up. Moog's quarterly earnings were spotty—the firm had rising annual earnings for the prior two years, and in most instances during that time quarterly earnings relative to the same quarter in the prior year (to account for seasonal adjustments) were rising, but in two instances out of eight they declined.

Lastly, the number of shares outstanding was checked to see if it was below 20 million, and Moog passed.

Moog is in the aerospace/defense industry and is a manufacturer of components and systems for the defense, commercial transportation (including Boeing and Airbus), and industrial markets.

The company suffered, along with the industry, from the cuts in defense spending. Its acquisition of Allied Signal's aerospace actuation business was, according to Value Line, expected to help existing product applications and open up opportunities with aircraft manufacturers.

Value Line also noted that its European operations were turning around, due to cost-control measures and a turnaround in the European market. However, these improvements were not expected to add to the bottom line for several quarters.

At the time of the screen, the company still faced risk from further declines in the defense budget.

Per Share Data and Financial Ratios

The first item of note is the fiscal year-end, which is October 1. The figures on the valuation worksheet (Figure 9-1), therefore, include all of Moog's 1994 fiscal year (based on a projection for the last quarter, made one month into the quarter).

The next item of note is the price trend. In 1992, both its high and low prices were considerably below those of the prior years; more recently, it had come back from that 1992 drop. This is one indication of its price momentum, not surprising given its relative strength trend, which had also risen since 1992.

On a longer-term basis, the price of the stock had dropped considerably from pre-1987 levels, from which it had yet to recover. For instance, in 1987 its high was $19.10 and its low was $8.00. Clearly the stock had been out-of-favor for quite some time.

Year-by-year earnings per share dropped substantially in 1992. They had started to trend up since then, reaching the 1990 level by mid-1994. That makes the five-year earnings growth rate -0.3%; the growth rate since the 1992 low was 43%. Value Line projected 1995 earnings per share of $1.30, most of which was due to its recent acquisition. However, Value Line expected earnings to continue to grow after 1995.

Figure 9-1: Valuation Worksheet

Company: MOOG Inc.   Current Price $ 9.13   Date (8 /31/ 94)

Ticker MOGA   Exchange ASE   Current P/E 16.0   Current Yield 0%

Financial Statement & Ratio Analysis

Per Share Information	Company 19 90	19 91	19 92	19 93	19 94	5-year avg	Industry or Competitor 19 94	5-year avg	Market 19 94
Price: High	10.00	9.50	7.60	9.80	9.60	9.30			
Price: Low	5.30	6.00	3.90	5.60	7.00	5.56			
Earnings per Share (EPS)	0.86	0.97	0.41	0.66	0.85	*growth rate:* −0.3%			
Dividends per Share (DPS)	0.00	0.00	0.28	0.00	0.00	*growth rate:* 0%			
Book Value per Share (BV)	11.66	12.93	12.62	11.99	12.55	12.35			
Financial Ratios									
Price-Earnings Ratio (P/E): Avg	8.9	8.0	14.0	11.7	9.8	10.5	11.0**	11.4***	
High *(High Price ÷ EPS)*	11.6	9.8	18.5	14.8	11.3	13.2			
Low *(Low Price ÷ EPS)*	6.2	6.2	9.5	8.5	8.2	7.7			

								2.8**	2.8***
Dividend Yield % (DY): Avg	0.0	0.0	0.0	0.0	5.4	0.0	0.0		2.8***
High (DPS ÷ Low Price)	0.0	0.0	0.0	0.0	7.2	0.0	0.0		
Low (DPS ÷ High Price)	0.0	0.0	0.0	0.0	3.7	0.0	0.0		
Payout Ratio % (DPS ÷ EPS)	0.0	0.0	0.0	0.0	68.3	0.0	0.0	34.0	32.2
Return on Equity % (EPS ÷ BV)	7.4	7.5	3.2	5.5	6.8	6.1		7.0	8.1
Financial Leverage* %	122	107	115	107	156	121		33	33

*long-term debt ÷ equity   **1992   ***1990 through 1993

Earnings-Based Valuation Estimates

Using historical growth rate to project 1995 EPS:

Average high P/E x estimated 19_95 EPS: 13.2 x 0.85 = $11.22   (high valuation estimate)

Average low P/E x estimated 19_95 EPS: 7.7 x 0.85 = $6.54   (low valuation estimate)

Using Value Line 1995 EPS estimate:

Average high P/E x estimated 19_95 EPS: 13.2 x 1.30 = $17.16   (high valuation estimate)

Average low P/E x estimated 19_95 EPS: 7.7 x 1.30 = $10.01   (low valuation estimate)

Except in 1992, the firm had paid no dividends. Value Line was not projecting any dividend payments over the next few years.

Book value per share had remained relatively steady, and the firm's book value at the time of the screen was at its five-year average.

In terms of financial ratios, Moog's September 1994 price-earnings ratio, at 16.0, was above its five-year average high. Clearly, the market's expectation for the firm was positive, based on a stronger outlook for future earnings.

Moog's dividend yield of 0% reflected its lack of dividend payments. The lack of dividend payments also produced a 0% payout ratio.

The 1994 return on equity for Moog of 6.8% was close to the industry average, a sign that the firm has been returning to its pre-1992 levels. Return on equity measures how well the firm is managed both operationally and financially. To boost return on equity, a company must increase its profits from sales, manufacture its goods more efficiently, or increase the level of financial leverage. Moog's use of financial leverage was way above the industry norm. In 1994, its financial leverage increased by 30%, reflecting the recent acquisition. It is unlikely that this resulted in the most recent increase in return on equity, since the acquisition occurred too recently; however it could be a cause of future increases in return on equity.

Valuing the Company

The bottom of the valuation worksheet (Figure 9-1) provides valuations using the earnings-based model. The dividend-based model is not used here, since no dividends have been paid.

For the earnings-based models, two valuations are provided: one using a 1995 earnings per share projection based on the five-year average growth rate of -0.3% (resulting in a 1995 EPS estimate of $0.85), and one using the Value Line 1995 earnings per share estimate (of $1.30). The five-year averages for the high and low price-earnings ratios were also used in the worksheet.

The valuation using the five-year average growth rate produced a range of $6.54 to $11.22; the valuation using the Value Line 1995 estimate produced a range of $10.01 to $17.16.

Moog's price in September of 1994 was $9.13. If Moog at this point were to continue its lackluster five-year average earnings growth record, it would appear to have been fairly priced based on the valuation model. But if it were turning around, as Value Line suggested it would have been a bargain. Clearly, a further understanding of the company—its products, competition, and market—would help in forming an opinion about the firm's outlook.

But the valuation worksheet suggested that the firm merited further investigation.

The basic approach used here adapts the stock winner characteristic rules in the initial screening phase, since it would be difficult to sort through a listing of stocks by hand and come up with those that best fit all the detailed trading rules in the original study. However, it is interesting to note how the firm stacks up according to those rules, and Table 9-2 does just that.

Conclusion

A careful examination of the assumptions is a critical part of the valuation and will help you identify factors that could be misleading in your final valuation.

While the worksheet examines quantitative factors, it is clear that many subjective factors go into the equation. To judge these factors, it is necessary to go beyond the statistics. Any final decision should be based on a better understanding of the company, its management, and its competitive environment. This can only be accomplished by a thorough reading of the firm's financial reports, as well as the reports and summaries on the firm and its industry.

Table 9-2: Stock Market Winners:
The Trading Rules and How Moog Stacked Up

Rules*	Did Moog Pass?
1. Price-to-book value less than 1.0	Yes. Current ratio: 0.72
2. Accelerating quarterly earnings—	
Consecutive Quarters	Yes. 19% between March and June; 44% expected between June and Sept.
Quarter-on-Quarter	Yes. 25% between June '94 & '93; 176% expected between Sept.'94 & '93
3. Positive 5-year earnings growth rate	No. Just slightly negative: -0.3%
4. Positive operating margin**	Yes. 12%
5. Relative strength rank of at least 70	Yes. 77%
6. Increase in relative strength rank	Yes. Rank of 52% one quarter prior
7. Stock selling within 15% of 2-year high	Yes. 93% of $9.80 2-year high
8. Fewer than 20 million shares outstanding	Yes. 7.7 million shares outstanding

*There were nine trading rules in the study, but one involves proprietary data and is excluded here.
**Operating margin substituted for pretax profit margin.

Adapting the Lynch Principles
to the Basic Approach

One of the best ways to learn about investing is to follow an example—preferably someone with a successful track record.

One popular investment guru, Peter Lynch, former portfolio manager of the Fidelity Magellan Fund has written two books that discuss the primary investment principles he followed when managing the ernormously popular fund. This chapter focuses on a basic approach that follows his rules-of-thumb for beating the pros.

The Lynch Principles

The Stock-Picking Checklist (see Table 10-1) summarizes the main principles outlined by Mr. Lynch in his two books, *One Up on Wall Street*, and *Beating the Street*.

Mr. Lynch advocates a "bottom-up approach," which means that you start your search process at the ground floor, looking for individual companies that appear to have promising products or services. Once you have identified a promising candidate, you then carefully research and analyze it, checking first to see if your initial impression is supported by financial evidence and the firm's competitive

Table 10-1: Stock Picking Checklist

• Invest only in industries and companies you understand and know the specific reason that you are buying the stock.	Your analysis should center on the factors that will move the stock price.
• How does the price-earnings ratio compare to the growth rate in earnings and dividends?	Look for low P/Es compared to earnings growth and dividend yield.
• How does the price-earnings ratio compare to its historical average?	Look for P/E in lower range of historical average.
• How does the price-earnings ratio compare to the industry?	Look for P/E below industry average.
• How stable and consistent are the earnings?	Study the pattern of earnings, especially how they react during a recession.
• How strong is the balance sheet?	Look for a low level of debt, especially bank debt.

- What is the cash position?

  Net cash per share should be high relative to stock price.

- Avoid hot companies in hot industries.

  Be wary of earnings growth rates above 50%

- Big companies have small moves, small companies have big moves.

  Small companies should be favored in your search because they have more upside potential.

- What is the level of industrial holdings?

  Look for low percentage of shares held by institutions and number of analysts following stocks.

- Are insiders buying the stock?

  Insider buying by a number of insiders is a positive sign.

- Is the company buying back shares?

  If so, this will support the stock price and probably indicates the company has been ignored, but management is confident.

environment, and then to see if the stock can be purchased at a reasonable price.

This process entails searching for candidates one-by-one, rather than beginning with a list of candidates that may have passed an initial screen. How do you find initial candidates? Mr. Lynch strongly advises that you put your own experience and knowledge to work, looking at companies with products and services with which you are familiar and thus more capable of analyzing.

Once you have found a promising candidate, he suggests that, among other things, you look for the following features:

- A price-earnings ratio relative to the earnings growth rate of less than 0.5
- A price-earnings ratio that is in the lower range of its historical average and below the industry average
- Stable and consistent earnings
- Low levels of debt

Other positive signs include: high net cash per share relative to the stock price; low levels of institutional holdings; insider buying by a number of insiders; and company share buy-backs. Mr. Lynch also favors smaller firms over larger firms, and dislikes "hot" stocks in "hot" industries.

Once you have spotted a promising candidate, the information source list in Table 10-2 can help you gather the information you need for further analysis. Many of these sources may be available in your local library. However, don't forget one of the single best sources of information—the company itself, from which you can request its financial reports. Table 10-2 also provides one pre-screened list that appears in the S&P Earnings Guide (firms that meet Mr. Lynch's low price-earnings ratio to growth rate rule-of-thumb)—you may find a firm or two listed there in which you are familiar with its product or service.

Once you have spotted a potential stock, the next step is an in-depth evaluation.

Intel Corp.: An Example

Intel Corp. offers an example of how a firm could be analyzed using the Lynch principles as a guide. Intel was selected because it appeared on the S&P Earnings Guide pre-screened list at the time of the analysis, in October of 1994—a sector quite familiar to at least one of the authors (John Bajkowski is editor of AAII's *Computerized Investing*).

John's summary of Intel in late 1994:

In late 1994, Intel was best known as the designer and manufacturer of the micro-processor or "brain" that drives most of the IBM-based personal computers. Intel's processors, controllers, and memory chips are also heavily used in communications, automation, and other electrical equipment.

Intel is, of course, a technology stock, a "hot" industry. Typically, the product life cycle within the industry is very short and getting shorter. Intel spent 11% of its $11 billion in sales on research and development to advance its products and keep one

Table 10-2: Promising Stock Candidates Information Sources

Pre-Screened List of Firms With Low P/Es Relative to Earnings Growth Rate

Standard & Poor's Earnings Guide (Monthly)—Includes summary (one-line) information and focuses on earnings and earnings growth estimates. The front periodically includes this list: *Strong EPS & Dividend to P/E Ratio:* These are firms whose 5-year annual earnings growth rate plus the current dividend yield relative to their price-earnings ratio is greater than 2. [Seeking firms which with a ratio above 2 is equivalent to the Peter Lynch rule uses the inverse formula—dividing the price-earnings ratio by the earnings growth rate—and seeks ratios below 0.5.] These firms also must pay dividends and have five years of positive earnings.

Lynch's Laws: Finding Information

Price Earnings Ratios, Earnings Growth, and Historical Earnings: The three most complete sources for historical corporate financial information are *Moody's Handbook of Common Stock, Standard & Poor's Stock Reports,* and the *Value Line Investment Survey.* In addition, don't forget the primary source—the company's own annual financial reports. Corporate annual reports will include both summary and detailed financial statements: the summaries cover a 5- or 10-year span. More detailed financial statements are available in the 10K. Both of these reports can be requested from the company.

Comparing Co. P/Es to Industry P/Es: S&P's *Industry Reports* provides a monthly review of 80 industries. In addition, data on industry indexes is provided in the *Wall Street Journal* (Dow Jones Industry Groups is presented daily), *Investor's Business Daily* (Industry Prices is presented every Tuesday), and *Barron's* (a listing of the Dow Jones Industry Groups is given in the Market Statistics Section). Value Line reports industry analysis sections, but these can be dated.

Balance Sheet Strength: All of the sources listed for price-earnings ratios and historical earnings are good sources for balance sheet strength.

Cash Position: All of the sources listed for price-earnings ratios and historical earnings are good sources for cash position. In addition, the monthly *S&P Stock Guide* reports current cash holdings, as well as long-term debt (Peter Lynch subtracts long-term debt per share from cash per share to determine a firm's net cash per share position.)

Level of Institutional Holdings: *Value Line's* full-page company summaries include a box called "Institutional Decisions" that reports the number of shares held by institutions. S&P's *Stock Guide* gives both the number of shares held by institutions holding shares in the company. S&P *Stock Reports* and *Moody's Handbook* also reports the percentage held by institutions.

Insider-Buying: *Value Line's* full-page company summaries include a box called "Insider Decisions" that reports insider buying.

Company Share Buybacks: *Value Line* often discusses buybacks in the write-up section. Also check in *Value Line* to see if the number of shares outstanding has been decreasing over time, an indication of company buybacks. Similar information is available in *S&P Stock Reports* and *Moody's Handbook.*

step ahead of its competitors. Intel is facing competition from competitors cloning its main processors and from a new generation of processor chips from companies such as IBM and Motorola. The chip business is very cut-throat, and Intel has used the court system, faster product introductions, and lower prices to meet the competition.

At that time of the analysis, Intel's future growth in earnings was dependent on greater volume of sales with lower profit margins, common to industries that reach a more mature phase. Intel at that time was pushing adoption of its latest generation chip, Pentium, at a much faster rate than earlier designs and rolling out more efficient plants to help keep costs down.

Per Share Information and Financial Ratios

Value Line was used as the primary source for financial information. Figures for 1994 were based on Value Line projections for the remainder of the year.

The first item of note is the price trend. Intel's stock price rose steeply and steadily from 1991 through 1993; in late 1994 it had since fallen from its 1994 high earlier in the year of $73.50.

Year-by-year earnings per share have steadily increased since 1990, with an average five-year growth rate of 38.6%. That certainly meets the Lynch rule of thumb of stable and consistent earnings; on the other hand, this high growth rate could put it in the "hot stock" category. More recently, however, earnings growth slowed: between 1993 and 1994, earnings went from $5.16 to $5.90 per share—an increase of 14%. Value Line predicted a continuation of that 14% growth rate, with a 1995 earnings per share projection of $6.75. Interestingly, this slowdown made Intel more appealing from the Lynch perspective—Intel may no longer have been the "hot" stock of several years ago.

Intel did not start paying dividends until 1992, when it paid a $0.05 dividend in the last quarter. Dividends were paid for the full year in both 1993 and 1994, during which dividends were increased from $0.20 to $0.22—a 10% increase. While that time span is too short to indicate any long-term trend, it did appear that Intel was committed to paying some level of dividends. Value Line estimates dividends per share of $0.27 in 1995. The fact that this firm started to pay dividends—and they were increasing—may have been another sign that this firm was moving away from its quick-growth phase and was starting to mature.

In terms of financial ratios, Intel's October 1994 price-earnings ratio, at 11.1, was below its five-year average high. Clearly, the market's expectation for the firm had dropped, based on its declining earnings growth rate. How did Intel's price-earnings ratio compare with the industry average? Value Line's price-earnings ratio for the industry was dated—1993 is the most recently reported figure.

Intel's price-earnings ratio was lower, however, than the 1994 industry average of 16.8 reported by S&P Industry Reports. With Intel's price-earnings ratio below its historical average and the industry average, it may have been an indication of under-valuation.

Intel's October 1994 dividend yield of 0.4% was so low that it is probably insignificant—no investor was buying this stock for the dividend.

The low level of dividends resuled in a very low payout ratio of 3.7% in 1994—below the industry average of 17.0%.

The 1994 return on equity of 25.1% for Intel was much higher than the industry average, and had increased over time, although it had slid back from its 1993 high of 28.8%.

Return on equity measures how well the firm is managed both operationally and financially. To boost return on equity, a company must increase its profits from sales, manufacture its goods more efficiently, or increase the level of financial leverage. Intel's use of financial leverage (long-term debt divided by equity) was far below the industry norm—its five-year average was 6.4% compared to an industry average of 17.2%. Intel therefore appeared to be maintaining its high return on equity from increasing sales—reflected in the year-by-year earnings increases.

What about some of the other Lynch Laws that are not found on the valuation worksheet? Using Value Line as a source, Intel violated most:

- Intel was not small—it had a market capitalization (419 million common shares outstanding
times $61.50 share price) of over $25 billion;
- It had a low level of net cash per share
relative to its stock price—its net cash per share
position was $4.59 (cash assets of $2,300 million less
$375 million in long-term debt, divided by 419
million common shares outstanding) compared to
its $61.50 per share stock price;
- Over 71% of its shares were held by institutions (298 million shares held by institutions divided by 419 million common shares outstanding);
- There had been no insider buying decisions
over the past year;
- No share buybacks were mentioned in the
Value Line company summary, and over time, the
number of shares outstanding has increased; and
- It was (and is) in a hot and highly competitive industry.

Valuing the Company

The bottom of the valuation worksheet (Figure 10-1)
provides valuations using both the earnings-based
model and the dividends-based model.

For the earnings-based models, the Value Line
estimate for 1995 earnings were used on the
worksheet, since this is a more conservative estimate. A projection based on Intel's five-year growth
rate of 38.6% would suggest 1995 earnings of $8.17;
however, given the slowdown in earnings growth,

Figure 10-1: Valuation Worksheet

Company: Intel Corp. Current Price $ 61.50 Date (9 /30 / 94)

Ticker INTC **Exchange** NMS **Current P/E** 11.1 **Current Yield** 0.4%

| | Financial Statement & Ratio Analysis | | | | | | Industry or Competitor | | Market |
| | Company | | | | | 5-year avg | 19 94 | 5-year avg | Current |
Per Share Information	19 90	19 91	19 92	19 93	19 94				
Price: High	26.00	29.60	45.80	74.30	73.50				
Price: Low	14.00	18.90	23.30	42.80	56.00				
Earnings per Share (EPS)	1.6	1.91	2.51	5.16	5.9	*growth rate:* 38.6%			
Dividends per Share (DPS)	0.00	0.00	0.05*	0.20	0.22	*growth rate:* 10%**			
Book Value per Share (BV)	8.99	10.83	13.01	17.94	23.55	14.86			
Financial Ratios									
Price-Earnings Ratio (P/E): Avg	12.5	12.7	13.8	11.3	11.0	12.3	14.4***	18.75†	18.0
High *(High Price ÷ EPS)*	16.3	15.5	18.2	14.4	12.5	15.4			
Low *(Low Price ÷ EPS)*	8.8	9.9	9.3	8.3	9.5	9.1			

							0.4***	0.5†	2.9
Dividend Yield % (DY): Avg	0.0	0.0	0.0	0.4	0.3	0.4**	0.4***	0.5†	2.9
High (DPS ÷ Low Price)	0.0	0.0	0.0	0.5	0.4	0.4**			
Low (DPS ÷ High Price)	0.0	0.0	0.0	0.3	0.3	0.3**			
Payout Ratio % (DPS ÷ EPS)	0.0	0.0	0.0	3.9	3.7	3.8**	17.0	13.0	
Return on Equity % (EPS ÷ BV)	17.8	17.6	19.3	28.8	25.1	21.7	10.0	12.5	
Financial Leverage %	9.6	8.2	4.6	5.7	3.8	6.4	15.1	17.2	

*one quarter only; **2-year figures; ***1993; †1990-1993.

Valuation Estimates

Model based on earnings (using Value Line 1995 EPS estimate):

Average high P/E × estimated 19 95 EPS: __15.4__ × __6.75__ = __$103.95__ (high valuation estimate)
Average low P/E × estimated 19 95 EPS: __9.1__ × __6.75__ = __$61.42__ (low valuation estimate)

Model based on dividends (using 1995 DPS estimate based on dividend growth rate):

Estimated 19 95 annual DPS ÷ average low DY: __0.24__ ÷ __0.003__ = __$80.00__ (high valuation estimate)
Estimated 19 95 annual DPS ÷ average high DY: __0.24__ ÷ __0.004__ = __$60.00__ (low valuation estimate)

Use decimal form for DY. For instance 5.4% would be 0.054.

this higher earnings projection is probably too optimistic.

Using the Value Line projections, the model produces a high valuation of $103.95 and a low valuation estimate of $61.42.

The dividend-based model uses a 1995 dividends per share projection of $0.24 based on the 10% increase over the past year. Although this time period does not indicate a trend, it does produce a more conservative estimate than the Value Line 1995 projection of $0.27. The dividend-based model produces a valuation range of $60.00 to $80.00. However, given the insignificant dividend yield paid by Intel, this model is less useful in valuing this stock—investors were not making decisions based on the dividend-paying capability of this firm, and therefore dividends were unlikely to play a significant role in the pricing of the stock.

Intel's October 1994 price of $61.50 was close to the low valuation indicated by the earnings-based model and suggested that the firm may have been undervalued. Intel also met some of the Lynch rules-of-thumb, but not all, as outlined above. These preliminary analyses suggested that the stock may merit further investigation but with some skepticism; certainly familiarity with the industry would be helpful.

Conclusion

A careful examination of the assumptions is a critical part of the valuation and will help you identify factors that could be misleading in your final valuation. While the worksheet examines quantitative factors, it is clear that many subjective factors go into the equation. To judge these factors, it is necessary to go beyond the statistics. Any final decision should be based on a better understanding of the company, its management, and its competitive environment. This can only be accomplished by a thorough reading of the firm's financial reports, as well as the reports and summaries on the firm and its industry.

Appendix A

Sources of Information

Almanac of Business and Industrial Financial Ratios
Published by Prentice Hall
Englewood Cliffs, NJ 07632
800/947-7700

Analyst Watch
Zack's Investment Research Inc.
155 N. Wacker Drive
Chicago, IL 60606
800/399-6659

Barron's
Dow Jones and Co.
200 Burnett Road
Chicopee, MA 01020
800/568-7625

Business Week
McGraw-Hill Inc.
P.O. Box 430
Hightstown, NJ 08520
800/635-1200

Dun & Bradstreet Industry Norms and Key Business Ratios
One Diamond Hill Rd.
Murray Hill, NJ 07974-0027
908/665-5224

Independent Investors Research Inc.
P.O. Box 12241
Research Triangle Park, NC 27709-2241
800/487-8625
919/847-2359

Industriscope
Media General Financial Services
P.O. Box 85333
Richmond, VA 23293
800/446-7922
804/649-6587

Investment Quality Trends
7440 Girard Ave., Suite 4,
La Jolla, CA 92037
619/459-3818

Investor's Business Daily
P.O. Box 66170
Los Angeles, CA 90066-8950
800/831-2525

Moody's
99 Church St.
New York, NY 10007
800/342-5647

Nelson's Earnings Outlook
One Gateway Plaza
Port Chester, NY 10573
800/333-6357

RMA Annual Statement Studies
Robert Morris Associates
1 Liberty Place
Philadelphia, PA 19103
215/851-0585

Standard & Poor's Corp.
25 Broadway
New York, NY 10004
800/221-5277

Standard & Poor's 500 Guide, annual Edition
Standard & Poor's MidCap 400 Guide, annual Edition
Standard & Poor's SmallCap 600 Guide, annual Edition
All are published by McGraw-Hill
13311 Monterey Ave.
Blue Ridge Summit, PA 17294
800/262-4729

The Wall Street Journal
Dow Jones & Company
200 Burnett Road
Chicopee, MA 01020
800/568-7625

Value Line Investment Survey
Value Line Publishing
220 E. 42nd Street
New York, NY 10017-5891
800/634-3583